Recreational Terror

SUNY Series, INTERRUPTIONS:
Border Testimony(ies) and Critical Discourse/s

Henry A. Giroux, editor

Recreational Terror

Women and the Pleasures of Horror Film Viewing

Isabel Cristina Pinedo

State University of New York Press

Published by
State University of New York Press, Albany

Printed in the United States of America

For information, address State University of New York Press, State University Plaza, Albany, N.Y., 12246

Production by Marilyn P. Semerad
Marketing by Theresa Abad Swierzowski

Library of Congress Cataloging-in-Publication Data

Pinedo, Isabel Cristina, 1957–
Recreational terror : women and the pleasures of horror film viewing / Isabel Cristina Pinedo.
p. cm. — (SUNY series, Interruptions — Border testimony(ies) and Critical Discourse/s)
Includes bibliographical references and index.
ISBN 0-7914-3441-9 (hc : acid-free paper). — ISBN 0-7914-3442-7 (pbk. : acid-free paper)
1. Horror films—History and criticism. 2. Motion picture audiences. 3. Motion pictures and women. I. Title. II. Series.
PN1995.9.H6P46 1997
791.43'616'082—dc21 97-8033
CIP

10 9 8 7 6 5 4 3 2 1

For Heather

CONTENTS

LIST OF ILLUSTRATIONS

ACKNOWLEDGMENTS

This project into the world of horror films started with an exploration into myself. As a child, monsters populated my world. Those I sought out in the day, on television and in stories, were welcome. Those that came to me in nightmares were not. It took a good chunk of my early adulthood to sort out the place of monsters in my life. Since then, some have become old friends, others I no longer need. If not for Jackie Dryfoos I might never have traveled the long, labyrinthine course that led me to understand and appreciate these strange and wondrous creatures. She kept me company when the traveling was hard and lit a candle in the dark. By being true, she showed me how to be true to myself.

Many friends and colleagues have contributed to the realization of this book. The members of my dissertation committee—Michael Brown, Stanley Aronowitz, Serafina Bathrick, and Tom Gunning—were invaluable in completing the project on which this book is based. I am grateful for Stanley's sweeping knowledge of theory which he generously shared with me, and Tom's attention to detail. Fina's theoretical and practical grasp of feminism was a delight, and it has been my privilege to be her colleague at Hunter College. Mike, the chair of my committee, provided unstinting support and remarkable acumen throughout my graduate school experience. His willingness to read this manuscript in its entirety, and to supply me with detailed comments on some portions of it were much appreciated.

As I began to conceive of this project, Marty Rubin generously commented on my writing and steered me towards feminist film theory, which I studied with Janet Staiger whose enthusiasm for the subject was infectious. I received incisive feedback on earlier drafts from the members of the Writing Group including Jo Anstey, Heather Levi, Melissa Orlie, Debbie Wuliger, and Lynn Chancer. Lynn generously commented on the entire manuscript. Her friendship and professional support has been a model to me of what it means to be a feminist, both personally and intellectually. Students in my Film and Society course at SUNY Purchase and in my Movies as Mass Communication course at Hunter College responded in thought-provoking ways to some of the material in this book. Two anonymous reviewers and Frank Tomasulo provided extremely helpful editorial suggestions on an earlier draft of chapter one, which was published in the *Journal of Film and Video*. Marian Meyers read and provided helpful comments on an earlier draft of chapter three. Lyell Davies generously read the whole manuscript and supplied encouraging remarks. Anne Rubenstein went above and beyond the call of duty sharing her copious and intelligent comments on the entire manuscript. Barry Davison provided much needed help with library research.

My thanks to Fairleigh Dickinson University for providing a faculty grant-in-aid in 1992 to assist with research expenses, and to Hunter College for a George N. Schuster Faculty Fellowship Grant in the Spring of 1995 to defray the costs of research and writing. I also benefitted from comments received on an earlier draft of chapter two, from the members of a CUNY Faculty Development Writing Seminar, Spring 1994. The Museum of Modern Art and stills archivist Terry Geesken assisted me in the selection of stills. Special thanks to my editors at SUNY Press, Priscilla Ross and Marilyn Semerad, for persevering with me through delays and complications.

A long, long time ago, in a galaxy far, far away, Tom Carr, despite his better judgment, went to see horror films with me. I am grateful to him and to other friends who have watched and discussed horror films with me, including Billy DiFazio,

Dawn Esposito, and Heather Levi. My special thanks to Heather who has read and encouraged every incarnation of this project. Her immeasurable love and support have been a mainstay of my life for many years. Her love of horror films has been but one of the many things we've shared in a relationship that has been vital to my well-being. Finally, I want to thank my mother and hero, Lucy Mettler, who taught me the importance of learning.

INTRODUCTION

Like others before me, my choice of book topic is intimately connected to who I am—a feminist and an avid horror fan—a combination some might regard as an oxymoron. Nevertheless, it is precisely my conflicting and evolving interests that have led me to treat this as an important topic of intellectual inquiry. Prior to my realization that the relationship between feminism and cinematic horror is an uneasy one, my interest in the horror film was strictly recreational.

Although the details of my background are not generalizable to the larger variegated population of horror fans, they do allow me to connect my interests to the larger social context of lived experience in which I participate. It is in this spirit that I share them here. I was raised in a Catholic, working-class, Latin American immigrant household, in a largely Italian neighborhood in the New York City borough of Queens. Until I reached graduate school, I was educated almost exclusively in Catholic schools where I experienced first the traditional church then the church of Vatican II. The visual and narrative imagery of this confluence of Catholicisms was a formative experience. I was fascinated by the narrative drama of Christ's torture and death, also known as The Passion. This story was ritually recounted in vivid detail on Good Friday when the priest recited the Stations of the Cross, fourteen episodes rehearsing Christ's lonely vigil in the Garden of Gethsemane, his betrayal, arrest, interrogation, lashing, crowning with thorns, ridicule, climb to Calvary, crucifixion and torment, culminating in his death on the cross. A stunning combination of bloody spectacle and excess-driven narrative.

This dense thicket of Catholic imagery prepared me for my childhood introduction to televised horror—*Twilight Zone, Outer Limits, Creature Feature, Night Gallery, Dark Shadows*, and the television runs of Universal and Hammer films. The English Gothics in particular dealt with such figures of the Catholic imagination as the Inquisition, witchcraft, the devil, magical incantations, and the saving power of holy water and the cross. What all these stories shared was the ability to provide me, and assorted family and friends, with legitimate occasions to overtly express terror and rage, feelings that were otherwise forbidden. These stories allowed us to exercise, rather than exorcise, emotions of tremendous importance that were otherwise denied legitimate expression.

As I grew up I discovered the novels of Stephen King, and followed the horror film into its later, gorier incarnations. Until, that is, my immersion into feminism in the early eighties placed me in the compromising position of being a fan of a genre which many feminists excoriated for its depiction of violence against women. My short-lived response to this quandary was to boycott the genre. The boycott ended when I decided that my desire to indulge, what had become by then, a guilty pleasure was stronger than my political qualms. Gradually, as I came to understand the powerful and salutary role that horror played in my life, I turned back to it in good conscience. This, in turn, led me to start questioning the critical and academic condemnation of the contemporary genre and to start formulating my own questions about the cultural significance of the horror genre's popularity. And so, the work that follows stems from the confluence of my early and ongoing engagement with the genre as a fan, my concern as a cultural analyst with the meaning of popular culture, and the contradictory position this puts me in as a feminist.

The horror genre has a long history in the United States, but I am more concerned with its contemporary forms, forms that I will argue exhibit postmodern characteristics. My concern with the postmodern dimension of horror does not revolve around the technology and mediatization themes that are so often addressed in discussions of postmodernism; instead I focus on representation and reception as sites of multiple and shifting identifications. This concern with postmodernism places me in yet another contradictory position since its relation to feminism is an uneasy one.* Although I explore the postmodern dimension of horror, feminism provides the frame of reference within which representation and reception are discussed.

My purpose in writing this is not to add specifically to the debates over postmodernism's place in contemporary society or its importance to social theory. Rather, I hope to use postmodernist themes and concepts to elucidate the horror genre. My embrace of postmodernist themes and concepts within a feminist framework is a way of keeping myself on my toes so that I do not succumb, to draw from the Catholic imagination, to the temptation to rescue the genre from knee-jerk disdain with my own brand of knee-jerk acceptance. My purpose here is not to condemn or rescue the genre but to open up the questions that consuming and analyzing horror films raises.

In the end, I decided to make the most of the contradictory positions this project puts me in. The questions that guide my work are well-suited to it, namely:

- What are the sources of the appeal of and meanings associated with the contemporary cinema of horror?
- What kind(s) of pleasure does consumption of these popular films yield?
- What can such a cultural object as the horror film tell us more generally about social life?

I present the problematic of the horror genre's appeal as contradictory from the outset. I am interested in understanding why the genre is such a powerful source of pleasure for me and for others, but especially for women. What does this say about us? How does it help us understand the social world in which we live? How does it help us to develop strategies for bringing about progressive social change? This seems like a lot to put on the shoulders of an entertainment form, but that,

I think, is one of the contributions that postmodernism makes to cultural studies in general, insofar as it challenges the distinction between high and low culture—in this case, the high culture of social theory and the low culture of commercial forms.

My concern with female spectatorship stems from several sources. One is the neglected place of theorizing female spectatorship in general. Second is the degree to which articles and books that do address themselves to spectatorship of horror have repeatedly avoided the issue of female spectatorship and therefore have exaggerated certain features of horror and ignored others. Third is my conviction that female subjectivity in the viewing of popular films is not only possible but a recurring experience. As a feminist, there are certain questions I must raise:

- What is most politically effective in bringing about a social transformation that will facilitate the widespread development of female agency, power, and self-determination?
- How does the contemporary horror genre contribute to this project? How does it detract from it?
- How does postmodernism contribute to this project, at least as it manifests itself in the horror genre? How does it disparage it?

As a feminist, I must raise these questions about female spectatorship. As a woman, they are ultimately questions about myself.

The autobiographical character of inquiry is always a factor in any research. The only difference is the degree to which that factor is perceived and acknowledged. The first week I spent revising an earlier draft of this book I felt excited. My pulse raced, the adrenaline rush propelled me to work, and I experienced enormous pleasure from the work. But by the end of the day I smelled of fear. Although I felt puzzled at the time, in retrospect it is not surprising that this experience of fear was a pleasurable one for me given the choice of my topic.

I loved horror films long before I perceived anything that I would today call postmodern. As a product of mass culture the horror film is not a utopian form; it is not a politically transformative experience in any grand sense of the term. However, my history with the genre has been a long and fruitful one, and it is for this reason that I explore its progressive potential, its positive effects, and its usefulness to feminists and to other people who may not call themselves feminist. I have endeavored throughout this book to conserve the tension between critical distance and passionate involvement in order to augment the power of my engagement with the genre.

Chapter 1 lays out five characteristics that together constitute the contemporary or postmodern horror genre. First, fictional horror constitutes a violent disruption of the everyday world. In postmodern horror, violence is a constituent element of everyday life and the threat of violence is unremitting. Second, it is the nature of fictional horror to transgress and violate all boundaries. Postmodern horror blurs the putative boundary between good and evil, normal and abnormal, and the outcome of the struggle is at best ambiguous. Danger to the social order is endemic. Third, horror throws into question the validity of rationality. Postmodern horror constructs a nihilistic universe in which causal logic collapses and one cannot rely on the efficacy of science or authority figures. Fourth, postmodern horror repudiates narrative closure. Narratives are apt to end apocalyptically with the defeat of the protagonists, or with incipient signs of a new unleashing. Finally, what makes these anxiety-inducing elements of fictional horror not only tolerable but pleasurable is the genre's construction of recreational terror, a simulation of danger that produces a bounded experience of fear not unlike a roller-coaster ride. Much as the horror film is an exercise in terror, it is simultaneously an exercise in mastery, in which controlled loss substitutes for loss of control. The proliferation of apocalyptic, graphically violent horror films which dot the post-sixties landscape attests to the need to express rage and terror in the midst of postmodern social upheaval.

In postmodern horror, the body figures as the site of this collapse. Chapter 2 explores further how recreational terror is produced in the postmodern horror film through the dialectic of showing and not showing, seeing and not-seeing the spectacle of the ruined body: at the level of the film, at the level of the audience, and at the institutional point of communication between the two known as the special-effects magazine, not being able to see structures the act of looking. Grounded in the desire to expose the hidden secrets of the flesh, the gore film provides an opportunity to investigate the similarities and differences between horror, the genre of the wet death, and pornography, the genre of the wet dream. I argue that a slippage occurs between these genres, both of which aim to affect the body of the viewer, and that this is what underlies the charge that violent horror films trigger violent behavior, a charge that overlooks the salient differences between the genres.

Much critical writing on the horror genre assumes that the pleasure associated with horror films belongs fundamentally to men. Chapter 3 examines the slasher film, and how its construction of recreational terror produces for female spectators a pleasurable encounter with violence and danger. It analyzes the tension between antifeminist elements, such as the stalking and murder of women, and feminist elements, such as the surviving female's ability and willingness to defend herself by any means necessary. As a woman who usurps the masculine prerogatives of aggression and the gaze, the surviving female shares an affinity with the lesbian. This is often what produces gender trouble for critics who read the surviving female as masculine, a reading I dispute. On the contrary, I argue that the slasher film creates an opening for feminist discourse by restaging the relationship between women and violence as not only one of danger in which women are objects of violence but also a pleasurable one in which women retaliate to become the agents of violence and turn the tables on their aggressors. The slasher film's potential for feminist discourse is exemplified in *The Stepfather*, a film which I analyze in some detail.

Not all postmodern horror films bring to fruition the feminist potential of the genre. But that is not to say that they are otherwise without a progressive aspect. Chapter 4 analyzes *Henry: Portrait of a Serial Killer* to demonstrate the central lesson of the postmodern horror film, namely that cloaked in a mantle of normalcy, chaos lies just beneath the surface ready to erupt at any moment. Monsters like Henry (or Freddy Krueger or Michael Myers) embody chaotic destructive forces that from the perspective of everyday life seem inexplicable and random. The irrepressibility and inevitability of violence represented in these films speak to the sense of helplessness that results when the normalcy of violence (be it the illegal varieties of street violence or state-sanctioned forms like corporate downsizing) is wrenched from its social context and made to seem extraordinary, unfathomable and inescapable. The postmodern horror film may not untangle the complex social forces that produce the violence we fear and the features of daily life that produce the violence we take for granted, but it does stage the terror and rage of a postmodern society with some honesty.

Different considerations apply when race is figured into the landscape of fictional horror. Chapter 5 analyzes several urban horror films that code the monster as a racial Other associated with a powerful and savage religion. Although these instances of race horror rely on the familiar equation of savagery with third-world peoples in a thinly-veiled expression of racism, there are countervailing tendencies within the subgenre, such as films that critically engage racism. Chapter 5 examines the interplay of these tendencies within that subgenre.

In the current climate of rabid political conservatism, I intend this analysis of the contemporary horror film to contribute to the debate over violence in films, women and violence, and popular culture. To rephrase Cyndi Lauper, girls don't just want to have fun, but fun deserves an honorable place at the table of a left transformative politics.

CHAPTER ONE

Recreational Terror and the Postmodern Elements of the Contemporary Horror Film

The universe of the contemporary horror film is an uncertain one in which good and evil, normality and abnormality, reality and illusion become virtually indistinguishable. This, together with the presentation of violence as a constituent feature of everyday life, the inefficacy of human action, and the refusal of narrative closure produces an unstable, paranoid universe in which familiar categories collapse. The iconography of the body figures as the site of this collapse. *Henry: Portrait of a Serial Killer* unfolds in this postmodern universe. The film, which details the sanguinary activities of a psychotic serial killer, was ready for release early in 1986 but remained on the distributor's shelf until 1989, when Errol Morris, director of *The Thin Blue Line* brought *Henry* to the Telluride Film Festival (*Village Voice* 1990, 59). Among the obstacles the film faced was the unwillingness of the Motion Picture Association of America (MPAA) to give it an *R* rating. The reason? Its "disturbing moral tone" (McDonough 1990, 59). Fearful because an *X* rating means death at the box office for nonpornographic films, distributors lost interest. Even the director John McNaughton expressed concern over whether the film would find an audience. As he told *Variety*, "[*Henry*] may be too arty for the blood crowd and too bloody for the art crowd" (quoted in Stein 1990, 59). McNaughton's concern and the MPAA's judgment rested on the film's tendency to play with and against the conventions of the contemporary horror genre. What makes it an innovative and daring film also makes it difficult to classify. This holds true as well for the postmodern horror film, of which *Henry* is emblematic.

The boundaries of any genre are slippery, but those of the postmodern horror film are particularly treacherous to negotiate since one of the defining features of postmodernism is the aggressive blurring of boundaries. How do we distinguish horror from other film genres and the postmodern horror film from other horror films? In this chapter I will argue that the contemporary horror genre, i.e., those horror films produced since about 1968, can be characterized as postmodern. I will formulate a working definition of the postmodern horror genre based on generalizations drawn from the study of films which cultural consensus defines as horror films, though not necessarily as postmodern ones.[1] In the course of delineating the postmodern features of the contemporary horror genre, I will differentiate it from its prior classical incarnation.

The Question of Postmodernism

In *Monsters and Mad Scientists: A Cultural History of the Horror Movie,* Andrew Tudor (1989) charts the development of the Anglo-American horror genre. The primary distinction he draws is between the pre-sixties (1931–1960) and the post-sixties (1960–1984) genre, terms that roughly correspond to my use of "classical" and "postmodern."[2] Tudor parenthetically aligns the post-1960s genre with postmodernism and the "legitimation crisis" of postindustrial society by which he means the failure of traditional structures of authority (1989, 222). Although Tudor does not involve himself in discussions of postmodernism per se, he does point out that the legitimation crisis of late capitalism may be the salient social context in which to ground the contradictions of the post-sixties horror genre. But before we can address the postmodern elements of the contemporary horror film, we must tackle the thorny issue of defining postmodernism.

Social theorists represent it as a widespread and elusive phenomenon, as yet unclearly defined, its amorphous boundaries are hard to pin down. Andreas Huyssen portrays it as both a historical condition and a style, "part of a slowly emerging cultural transformation in Western societies, a change in sensibility" (repr. 1990, 234). Todd Gitlin associates postmodernism with the erosion of universal categories, the collapse of faith in the inevitability of progress, and the breakdown of moral clarities (1989, 353). Jean-François Lyotard characterizes the postmodern as entailing a profound loss of faith in master narratives (claims to universal Truth) and disenchantment with the teleology of progress (1984, xxiv). Craig Owens identifies it with "a crisis of [Western] cultural authority" (1983, 57).

For my purposes, the postmodern world is an unstable one in which traditional (dichotomous) categories break down, boundaries blur, institutions fall into question, Enlightenment narratives collapse, the inevitability of progress crumbles, and the master status of the universal (*read* male, white, monied, heterosexual) subject deteriorates. Consensus in the possibility of mastery is lost, universalizing grand theory is discredited, and the stable, unified, coherent self acquires the status of a fiction. Although the political valence of postmodernism is subject to debate, there is much to be said for the progressive potential of this paradigm shift.

Clearly, the term *post*modernism acknowledges a shift from modernism, one not clearly defined and unable to stand as a separate term. But this cultural transformation was not ushered in by an apocalyptic ending or a clean break. It was and continues to be a matter of uneven development, where, to heed a warning issued by postmodernists, development cannot be conflated with progress. Insofar as we can conceptualize this cultural transformation as a break, it might be more fruitful to speak of it as a stress break, not the result of an originary traumatic event but the cumulative outcome of repetitive historical stresses including the Holocaust, Hiroshima, the Cold War, Vietnam, the anti-war movement, and the various liberation movements associated with the sixties: civil rights, black power, feminism, and gay liberation. Indeed, the impetus to situate postmodernism as a sixties or post-sixties phenomenon lies in the celebrated (or scorned) association of that period with cultural contradictions and resistance to authority that figure so prominently in discussions of the postmodern today.

The Relationship of Postmodernism to Popular Culture

The contemporary horror genre is sometimes criticized in modernist terms for being aligned with the degraded form of pleasure-inducing mass culture. Critics relegate the contemporary genre to the ranks of ideologically conservative culture and excoriate or laud it for promoting the status quo through its reinforcement of such classical binary oppositions as normal/abnormal sexuality. Indeed, in *Dreadful Pleasures* (1985), James Twitchell portrays the horror film as a morality tale that demonstrates the dangers of sexuality outside the heteromonogamous nuclear family.

In contrast, the vexed relationship of the contemporary horror film to postmodernism is rarely articulated. When the contemporary genre is associated with postmodernism it is often to discredit one or both. For Kim Newman, "the postmodern horror film" refers to those eighties horror films characterized by camp. This comic turn signals for Newman a degeneration, a dying out of the genre's capacity to depict "the horrors and neuroses of the age," a function he claims is necessary to culture but one that has been displaced and dispersed across other genres that are themselves increasingly hybrid in form (1988, 211–15). He speaks as a disappointed horror fan for whom "postmodern horror films" fail to do what they are fitted to do. Tania Modleski, on the other hand, is no fan of the genre. In "The Terror of Pleasure: The Contemporary Horror Film and Postmodern Theory," she classifies contemporary horror films as an expression of postmodernism and concludes that the former illustrate what is most perverse about the latter. This position bears closer inspection.

Although in principle postmodernism erodes all binary oppositions, Huyssen locates postmodernism's defining feature in its challenge to modernism's grounding distinction between high (artworld) culture and low (mass) culture. Postmodernism blurs the boundaries between art and mass culture. Ironically, as both Huyssen (repr. 1990, 241) and Modleski (1986, 156) argue, many postmodernists unselfconsciously reproduce the high culture/low culture opposition in its modernist Frankfurt School form in their own work. They say, in effect, that mass culture produces pleasure, which inscribes the consumer into the dominant bourgeois ideology. In contrast, the decentered text produces *jouissance* and takes an adversarial stance against bourgeois society. Modleski aligns the contemporary horror film with the latter form but questions its value for feminism.

Modleski identifies the following as postmodern elements of the contemporary horror film: open-ended narratives, minimal plot and character development, and (relatedly) the difficulty of audience identification with undeveloped and unlikeable characters. Modleski argues that the decentered, disordered horror film, like the avant-garde, changes textual codes in order to disrupt narrative pleasure, and that as such it is a form of oppositional culture. (Huyssen notes that postmodernism appropriates and recyles many of modernism's aesthetic strategies, like the ones Modleski indicates.) Modleski aligns the horror film with postmodernism and both with the disruption of pleasure in order to question the political wisdom of renouncing pleasure for women, given the lengths to which women have historically been denied pleasure, and consequently to question the limits of postmodernism for feminism.

Modleski raises important questions. But her depiction of the contemporary horror film is flawed and therefore her conclusion is flawed. She fails to grasp the ways in which the contemporary horror film *is* pleasurable, not only for a male audience but also for a female audience. Although the horror film is not necessarily critical or radical, it does contain, as Huyssen suggests for postmodernism, "productive contradictions, perhaps even a critical and oppositional potential" (repr. 1990, 252).

But before embarking on this exploration, I want to address the apparent contradiction contained in the notion of a postmodern genre. The classical genres are defined as bounded by preestablished rules. Genre theory seeks to elucidate these rules and thus provide unity and coherence to a group of films.

In contrast, a postmodern work breaks down boundaries, transgresses genres, and is characterized by incoherence. A postmodern genre would seem to be an oxymoron. So what does it mean to talk about a postmodern genre, especially given that "genre" is a structural idea? First, the notion of transgression presupposes existing genres to be transgressed (Cohen 1988). The postmodern horror film transgresses the rules of the classically oriented horror genre, but in doing so it also retains some features of the classical genre such that it is possible to see and appreciate the transgression. Furthermore, the postmodern horror film draws upon other generic codes and structures, in particular, science fiction and the suspense thriller, to concoct hybrids like science-fiction horror, of which *Alien* (1979) is a notable example. Thirdly, since a genre is in part constituted by audience expectations, a degree of license is granted to the horror film as incoherence and violation enter the narrative and visual lexicon of the genre audience through repeated viewings. Indeed, the genre audience acquires a taste for the destructuring tendency of the contemporary horror film, and a willingness not to resist it. Consequently, the genre audience greets a new horror film with the expectation of being surprised by a clever overturning of convention.

Although in practice there is overlap between the classical and postmodern forms of the genre, as there must be, analytically it is fruitful to draw this distinction in order to perceive the changes that have transpired between the emergence of the Hollywood horror film of the thirties and the films of the nineties. In doing so, it is important to bear in mind that the shift from classical to postmodern paradigms does not entail a clean, historically definable break. It is, rather, a process of uneven development in that each film both uses and departs from rules and that this process does not itself follow clear and definite rules.

Classical and Postmodern Paradigms of the Horror Genre

The classical horror film is exemplified in films such as *Dracula* (1931), *Frankenstein* (1931), and *Dr. Jekyll and Mr.*

Hyde (1931). The creature feature films of the post-war period—including *The Thing* (1951), *Invasion of the Body Snatchers* (1956), and *The Blob* (1958)—share a similar narrative structure, which Tudor lays out. The film opens with the violent disruption of the normative order by a monster, which can take the form of a supernatural or alien invader, a mad scientist, or a deviant transformation from within. The narrative revolves around the monster's rampage and people's ineffectual attempts to resist it. In the end, male military or scientific experts successfully employ violence and/or knowledge to defeat the monster and restore the normative order (Tudor 1989, 81–105).[3] The boundary between good and evil, normal and abnormal, human and alien is as firmly drawn as the imperative that good must conquer evil, thus producing a secure Manichean worldview in which the threats to the social order are largely external and (hu)man agency prevails, largely in the figure of the masterful male subject. As Robin Wood notes, the films of the thirties further distanced their monsters from everyday life by locating them in an exotic time or place (1986, 85).

In the fifties, the gothic monsters largely receded into the background,[4] and what emerged was an amalgam of science-fiction and horror elements known as the creature feature. This hybrid combines science fiction's focus on the logically plausible (especially through technology) with horror's emphasis on fear, loathing, and violence. The fifties films generally locate the monster in a contemporary American city, sometimes a small town, thus drawing the danger closer to home, but they retain the exotic in the monster's prehistoric or outer space origins (Lucanio 1987, 36–37).

The postmodern horror film is exemplified by films such as *Night of the Living Dead* (1968), *The Texas Chain Saw Massacre* (1974), *Halloween* (1978), *The Thing* (1982), *A Nightmare on Elm Street* (1984), and *Henry: Portrait of a Serial Killer* (1990). Again, drawing on Tudor's analysis we can summarize the narrative structure as follows. Such films usually open with the violent disruption of the normative order by a monster, which can take the form of a supernatural or alien invader, a deviant transformation from within, a psychotic, or a combination of these forms. Like its classical predecessors, the postmodern horror film revolves around the monster's graphically violent rampage and ordinary people's ineffectual attempts to resist it with violence. In the end, the inefficacy of human action and the repudiation of narrative closure combine to produce various forms of the open ending: the monster triumphs (*Henry*); the monster is defeated but only temporarily (*Halloween*), or the outcome is uncertain (*Night of the Living Dead, Texas Chain Saw Massacre, The Thing, Nightmare on Elm Street*). The boundary between living and dead, normal and abnormal, human and alien, good and evil, is blurred, sometimes indistinguishable. In contrast to the classical horror film, the postmodern film locates horror in the contemporary everyday world, where the efficacious male expert is supplanted by the ordinary victim who is subjected to high levels of explicit, sexualized violence, especially if female. Women play a more prominent role as both victims and heroes. The postmodern genre promotes a paranoid worldview in which inexplicable and increasingly internal threats to the social order prevail (Tudor 1989, 81–105).

Key elements of the transition from classical to postmodern paradigms are played out in *Targets* (1968), a self-reflexive film that juxtaposes the gothic monster of the classical paradigm with the psychotic monster of the postmodern paradigm. *Targets* is about a clean-cut, normal-seeming, suburban young man, Bobby Thompson, who inexplicably kills his wife and mother, then snipes at freeway motorists from a water tower. (Thompson's character is based on Charles Whitman who went on a murder spree in Austin, Texas in 1966.) A parallel plot features Boris Karloff as an aging horror film star who decides to retire because he has become anachronistic. People are no longer terrified by his films. Why should they be, when the headlines of everyday life are more horrific? The two narrative lines intersect when Thompson snipes from behind the screen of a drive-in theater at an audience watching *The Terror*, a 1963 gothic horror film featuring Boris Karloff. The juxtaposition of these two figures dramatizes how the psychotic killer's inexplicable violent rampage has supplanted the traditional monster of castles and closed endings.

Characteristics of the Postmodern Horror Genre

Despite the enormous breadth of films falling under the rubric of horror, there are identifiable elements that define horror in general, classical horror, and postmodern horror. I locate five characteristics that *operate together* to constitute the postmodern horror film:

1. Horror constitutes a violent disruption of the everyday world.
2. Horror transgresses and violates boundaries.
3. Horror throws into question the validity of rationality.
4. Postmodern horror repudiates narrative closure.
5. Horror produces a bounded experience of fear.

The first four traits refer to the workings of the film text; the fifth refers largely to the dynamic between the film and the audience. The first three apply to both classical and postmodern paradigms but operate differently in each. The fourth trait is particular to the postmodern paradigm. The fifth applies to horror in general, though I will discuss how it applies specifically to postmodern horror. Each characteristic operates in the *context* of the others; none is constitutive of the genre in and of itself. But together they form an interlocking web that constitutes the genre. This is a working definition, not an exhaustive list of qualifying criteria, and as such, this provisional definition is subject to the ongoing historical changes of the genre. The postmodern genre operates on the principles of disruption, transgression, undecidability and uncertainty.

Horror Constitutes a Violent Disruption of the Everyday World

Contrary to popular criticism, violence in the horror film is not gratuitous but is rather a constituent element of the genre. The horror narrative is propelled by violence, manifested in both the monster's violence and the attempts to destroy the monster. Horror is produced by the violation of what are tellingly called natural laws—by the disruption of our presuppositions about the integrity and predictable character of objects, places, animals, and people. Violence disrupts the world of everyday life; it explodes our assumptions about normality. The impermeability of death is violated when corpses come back to life (*Dracula* [1931], *Night of the Living Dead* [1968]). The integrity of self is breached when the body undergoes a radical transformation (*Dr. Jekyll and Mr. Hyde* [1931], *The Fly* [1986]).

The horror film throws into question our assumptions about reality and unreality. Like Harold Garfinkel's disruption experiments, it treats "an important state of affairs as something that it 'obviously,' 'naturally,' and 'really,' is not" (1967, 50). It disorients the viewer's taken-for-granted reality. Horror violates our assumption that we live in a predictable, routinized world by demonstrating that we live in a minefield, by demanding a reason to trust in the taken-for-granted realm of "ordered normality."

In the classical paradigm, the violent disruption is often located in or originates from a remote, exotic location. In contrast, the postmodern paradigm treats violence as a constituent element of everyday life. As Gregory Waller puts it, "the entire [contemporary horror] genre is an unsystematic, unresolved exploration of violence in virtually all its forms and guises" (1987, 7). The disruption takes the form of physical violence against the body: (typically nonsexual) invasion of body cavities or of body surfaces to create cavities, the release of body fluids through stabbing and slashing, the tearing of body parts from each other, the wrenching transformation of bodies. Gore—the explicit depiction of dismemberment, evisceration, putrefaction, and myriad other forms of boundary violations with copious amounts of blood—takes center stage.

The postmodern paradigm is characterized by the forceful importance of what Philip Brophy[5] calls the act of *showing* the spectacle of the ruined body. In contrast, the classical paradigm focuses on the more circumspect act of *telling* (1986, 8). This difference in the approach to violence is one of the primary distinctions between the classical and postmodern paradigms. The latter's fascination with the spectacle of the mutilated body, the creative death, necessitates its high level of explicit violence and privileging of the act of showing. The dismembered body, the body in bits and pieces, occupies center stage in the postmodern paradigm. Pete Boss, following Brophy, claims that the primacy of *body horror* is central to the contemporary horror genre, which he too characterizes as postmodern. Characteristically, everything else, including narrative and character development, is subordinated to "the demands of presenting the viewer with the uncompromised or privileged detail of human carnage" presented in an emotionally detached manner so that what fascinates is not primarily the suffering of the victim but her or his bodily ruination (Boss 1986, 15-16).

Body horror can be accomplished with only a part of the body standing in for the mutilated whole. Such a scene appears in *A Nightmare on Elm Street*, a film in which a burn-scarred supernatural killer stalks teenagers in their dreams and the lethal violence he inflicts there is actually inscribed on their bodies. Glen, against the advice of his perspicaciously discerning girlfriend Nancy, falls asleep in his bed. As he does, the killer's arms reach up from inside the bed and yank him into it in a sucking motion. He vanishes. After a pause, a geyser of blood shoots up from the bed to the ceiling. In defiance of gravity, blood flows in waves along the ceiling, out to the walls. Although the mutilated body per se is withheld from view the frame is focused on the eruption of blood whose copiousness far exceeds the contents of the missing body. In the postmodern genre, violence can burst upon us at any time, even when we least expect it, even when the sun is shining, even in the safety of our own beds, ravaging the life we take for granted, staging the spectacle of the ruined body. The postmodern genre is intent on imaging the fragility of the body by transgressing its boundaries and revealing it inside out.

Horror Transgresses and Violates Boundaries

Although violence is a salient feature of the genre, it must be situated in the context of monstrosity, culturally defined as an unnatural force. As Stephen Neale remarks,

FIGURE 1.1. Postmodern horror disrupts our presuppositions about the integrity and predictable character of things by showing bodily transgressions. From *A Nightmare on Elm Street* (1984), courtesy of Museum of Modern Art Film Stills Archive.

> what defines the specificity of [the horror] genre is not the violence as such, but its conjunction with images and definitions of the monstrous. What defines its specificity with respect to the instances of order and disorder is their articulation across terms provided by categories and definitions of "the human" and "the natural." (1980, 21)

Horror violates the taken-for-granted "natural" order. It blurs boundaries and mixes categories that are usually regarded as discrete to create what Mary Douglas (1966) calls "[im]purity and danger." The anomaly manifests itself as the monster: a force that is unnatural, deviant, and possibly malformed. The monster violates the boundaries of the body in a two-fold manner: through the use of violence against other bodies as discussed above and through the disruptive qualities of its own body. The monster's body is marked by the disruption of categories; it embodies contradiction. The pallor of the vampire, the weirdly oxymoronic "living dead" signifies death, yet the sated vampire's veins surge with the blood of its victim. The monster disrupts the social order by dissolving the basis of its signifying system, its network of differences: me/not me, animate/inanimate, human/nonhuman, life/death. The monster's body dissolves binary differences.

Horror indiscreetly mixes categories to create monsters. According to Noel Carroll (1990; 43, 46) monsters can take the form of either fusion or fission figures. A fusion figure combines contradictory elements in an unambiguous identity. Examples include composite figures of life and death (the creature in *Frankenstein* [1931]; the zombies in *Night of the Living Dead* [1968]), self and other (the scientist-fly in *The Fly* [1958], the demonically possessed girl in *The Exorcist* [1973]). In contrast, a fission figure combines contradictory elements in two identities connected over time by the same body. Examples include the temporally sequential combination of human and werewolf (*I Was a Teenage Werewolf* [1957], *The Howling* [1981]), human and alien (*Invasion of the Body Snatchers* [1956], *The Thing* [1982]).

The fusion and fission figures of postmodern horror assume overtly sexual proportions. The woman who bears

The Brood (1979) produces an external womb, a birth sac that hangs from her abdomen. The male protagonist of *Videodrome* (1983) develops a vaginal slit in his abdomen which is forcibly penetrated with a videotape. This figure combines not only male and female but organic and inorganic matter, giving new meaning to the term wetware. In *Dr. Jekyll and Sister Hyde* (1971), the good doctor's infamous transformation involves a sex change.[6]

The monster signifies what Julia Kristeva calls the "abject," that which does not "respect borders, positions, rules"—"the place where meaning collapses" (1982, 4, 2).[7] Danger is born of this confusion because it violates cultural categories. This is why the destruction of the monster is imperative; it is only when the monster is truly dead and subject to decay that it ceases to threaten the social order. Disintegration promises to reduce the monster to an undifferentiated mass, one that no longer embodies difference and contradiction, for "where there is no differentiation, there is no defilement" (Douglas 1966, 160).

Although classical and postmodern paradigms of the genre share most of the foregoing characteristics, they differ in two important respects: the nature of their moral universe and the resolution of conflict. The classical paradigm draws relatively clear boundaries between the contending camps of good and evil, normal and abnormal, and the outcome of the struggle almost invariably entails the destruction of the monster. Although boundary violations are at issue in classical horror, repairs can be effected. Good triumphs over evil; the social order is restored. In contrast, the postmodern paradigm blurs the boundary between good and evil, normal and abnormal, and the outcome of the struggle is at best ambiguous. Danger to the social order is endemic.

Nothing is what it seems to be in postmodern horror. Take, for instance, *A Nightmare on Elm Street*, a film about a nightmare in which the protagonist, Nancy, dreams she wakes up only to find herself propelled into yet another terrifying dreamscape right up to the conclusion of the film. In this postmodern scene, the referent or "reality" is gone, and she is caught within a closed system from which there is no exit. It is thus that the postmodern horror genre operates on the principle of undecidability.

This principle is extended from the narrative level to the cinematographic level. The postmodern horror film repeatedly blurs the boundary between subjective and objective representation by violating the conventional cinematic (lighting, focus, color, music) codes that distinguish them. This is one reason that the dream-coded-as-reality occupies a privileged position within the postmodern horror genre. Another is its close association with the unconscious and the irrational.

Horror Throws into Question the Validity of Rationality

Horror exposes the limits of rationality and compels us to confront the irrational. The realm of rationality represents the ordered, intelligible universe that can be controlled and predicted. In contrast, the irrational represents the disordered, ineffable, chaotic, and unpredictable universe which constitutes the underside of life. In horror, irrational forces disrupt the social order. The trajectory of the classical narrative is to deploy science and force (often together as when science is put into the service of the military) to restore the rational, normative order, whereas the postmodern narrative is generally unable to overcome the irrational, chaotic forces of disruption. Because of this narrative structure, the classical paradigm's critique of science is necessarily limited. It takes the form, as in *Frankenstein*, of the hubris-inspired overreacher who aspires to be like God. Or the form of military science gone awry as in *Them!* (1954) in which exposure to radiation causes ants to mutate into giants. The postmodern paradigm's critique of science and rational discourse runs much deeper, as I will show. But first, I want to consider how horror in general questions the validity of rationality.

Horror films assert that not everything can or should be dealt with in rational terms. As the parapsychologist warns the rational skeptic in *The Haunting* (1963), "the supernatural is something that isn't supposed to happen, but it does happen . . . if it happens to you, you're liable to have that shut door in your mind ripped right off its hinges." Indeed, mental doors are ripped off their hinges in *A Nightmare on Elm Street,* a film in which teenagers who dream about Fred Krueger can be killed by him in their dreams. Nancy pops caffeine pills and coffee by the potful because she is "into survival." Ultimately, she survives because she rejects the rational belief that dreams are not real and instead puts her faith in an irrational premise that collapses dream and reality. Her boyfriend Glen, however, lulls himself into a false sense of security. After all, he is home in bed, his parents are downstairs, and he is surrounded by stereo and television. His complacency, despite Nancy's repeated warnings, allows him to fall asleep, with fatal consequences.

Characters who insist upon rational explanations in the face of evidence that does not lend itself to rationality are destined to become victims of the monster. In *The Thing* (1951), the rational skeptic is Dr. Carrington, a scientist who seeks to communicate with the alien, a plant-based life form, who as a creature capable of space travel represents for him a member of an intelligent species. He is injured when he tries to reason with the creature. The rational skeptic, usually male, is punished or killed for his epistemological recalcitrance. Since science constitutes itself as a masculine enterprise, it is not surprising that the doomed rational skeptic tends to be male. The ones who survive necessarily suspend their rational presuppositions and trust their gut instincts.

In horror films, unlike the fairy tale, the monster is usually irrational and impervious to the request to sit down and reason together.[8] The monster's violence runs its own inexorable course. Although the monster is not susceptible to reason or propitiation, it is susceptible to violence. Characters who survive must come to terms not only with the irrationality of the situation but also with their own ability to be as single-mindedly destructive as the monster. In *A Nightmare on Elm Street,* Nancy learns that during her childhood, Fred Krueger, a child murderer who was freed on a technicality, was burned to death in a boiler room—the dark and dank site of his crimes and of the teenagers' nightmares—by a vigilante party of outraged parents, including her own. Krueger's body bears the mark of that violence. His teeth are charred; his skin is raw, burned, and seems to ooze a viscous substance. He is avenging himself by slaughtering the teenage children of those parents. Nancy learns that Krueger is the legacy of parental violence, and that she too is capable of wielding violence to defend herself.

In horror, the narrative is propelled by violence, not only by the monster's violence but by the protagonist's. To be efficacious, the protagonist must objectify the monster and subject it to a controlling gaze; that is, she must treat it the way it treats her. Paradoxically, characters who survive in horror films eschew critical tenets of rationality (for instance, that the attacker cannot be dead already), while at the same time they utilize instrumental rationality to objectify the monster and facilitate their own exercise of violence. Postmodern horror compels its heroes, many of whom are women, to both exercise instrumental rationality and to rely on intuition; it requires them to be both violent and to trust their gut instincts. As such, postmodern horror defies the Cartesian construction of reason that reduces it to instrumental rationality and pits it against emotion and intuition. According to the Cartesian construction of reason, rationality is masculine, associated with mastery, and requires the domestication of irrationality, which is feminine and associated with the body and disorder (Di Stefano 1990, 68). This limited conception of reason disparages the feminine. Postmodern horror combines, in the (often female) figure of the hero, instrumental rationality and intuition.

Cops and psychiatrists (descendants of the soldiers and scientists of classical horror) are largely absent from or ineffectual in the postmodern genre, despite the latter's insistence on the use of force. When experts are called in, they are not likely to be effective. For instance, in *The Entity* (1982) a woman is tormented by a phantom rapist. When psychiatry proves to be of no avail, she turns to parapsychology, which though more appropriate, is equally unable to extricate her. In the end, the inefficacy of science leaves the horror of her predicament unabated.

The nihilistic universe of postmodern horror cannot rely on the efficacy of science or authority figures. In *Halloween*, Michael Myers escapes from an insane asylum to return to his hometown where he will reenact the murder of his sister. The psychiatrist, who after fifteen years of observation can only pronounce that Michael is "simply and purely EVIL," teams up with the local police to track him down. To emphasize the futility of the law, we are shown Michael driving directly past the psychiatrist (who has his back to the street and is waiting for the police officer) without any hint of apprehension on Michael's part, nor any recognition on the part of the law.

The postmodern horror film throws into question two of the basic principles underpinning Western society: temporal order and causal logic. In *A Nightmare on Elm Street*, there is a glaring discrepancy between the explicit focus on time—the radio announces it, the characters set deadlines by the clock, and the alarm clock goes off at previously discussed times—and the implied duration of the narrative events taking place in those time frames. It is midnight when Glen is killed—the death scene itself lasts about three minutes—and 12:09 by the time police and ambulance are on the scene. (The six-minute speed with which police and ambulance respond to a distress call in a middle-class suburban neighborhood may be plausible, but especially in the context of ensuing events, it does strain credibility.) Between 12:10 and 12:20, Nancy sets up two elaborate booby traps—including piercing a hole in a light bulb and filling it with gun powder, installing a bolt lock on a door, rigging up a hammer to fall when the door is opened, setting a trip wire—and still has time to have a heartfelt talk with her mother. Time is unhinged, and this adds to the dreamlike texture of the film. One scene in particular resonates with nightmare imagery: Nancy flees from Krueger and runs up the stairs. The steps collapse like marshmallows beneath her feet, as she struggles laboriously to run but can only move in slow motion.

Causal logic also collapses in the postmodern horror film; thus, there is no explanation for the murders, cannibalism, dismemberment, and violence that take place in *The Texas*

Chain Saw Massacre. Despite the documentary claims in the prologue, the film not only fails to provide an explanation of events, but even language collapses in the final thirty minutes of the film. The lengthy sequence in which Sally is pursued, captured, tortured, and escapes is dominated by the sound of the chain saw; her relentless screams, groans, and pleas; the killers' taunts, bickering, laughter, and mutterings; and an ominous soundtrack. The few lines of dialogue serve not to anchor us in the rational but to demonstrate how demented the killers are.[9]

The postmodern horror film constructs a nihilistic universe in which the threat of violence is unremitting. *Night of the Living Dead* opens with Barbra and Johnny on a mundane trip to a rural cemetery to lay flowers on the grave of a dead, but still guilt-exacting, father. This prosaic event takes a horrific turn when Barbra is attacked by a zombie.[10] Her brother fights to save her but is quickly overcome. Distraught, she flees to the relative safety of a farmhouse where she encounters Ben (and later other refugees) and retreats into silence. Between the time that Barbra is attacked and the time that she encounters Ben—a seven minute sequence—there is no dialogue, only screams, thunder, and background music. The collapse of speech occurs not only here but also in the zombies' utter silence, and in the inability of the human characters to communicate with each other, from the quarrelsome relationship between Barbra and Johnny to the unhappily married Coopers who bicker contemptuously throughout the crisis, from Barbra's semicatatonic state through most of the film to the running feud between Ben and Harry Cooper for leadership.

The small group is beseiged by an unrelenting and ever-growing mob of zombies who brutally kill and cannibalize the living. The newly dead corpses then proceed to metamorphose into zombies and join in the onslaught. Thus, toward the end of the film, the dead daughter savagely kills and consumes the mother who tended her wounds.

The human survivors use first a radio, then a television to try to make sense of their predicament, to learn what the authorities know, and to formulate a plan of action. The newscaster describes the crisis as an "epidemic of mass murder" engulfing part of the country "with no apparent pattern or reason." The "flesh-eating ghouls" are characterized as both "ordinary-looking people" and "misshapen monsters" from whom "no one is safe." Law enforcement officials seem completely bewildered.

In postmodern horror, causal logic collapses even when the narrative entertains a logical explanation for the chaos. Thus, a newscaster speculates that a Venus probe that carried high-level radiation back to Earth may be responsible for the dead rising from their graves. What locates this "scientific" account in the realm of horror rather than science fiction is the insignificant role rational discourse plays in the film and the film's sustained focus on the mutilation of the body. Indeed, the film's attention to body horror earned it the charge of being "an unrelieved orgy of sadism" by *Variety* (quoted in McCarty 1990, 103).

The running rational argument in *Night of the Living Dead* concerns whether to fortify the main body of the house, which provides multiple escape (or invasion) sites, or to take cover in the barricaded cellar. Ben, the hero, advocates—and convinces most of the others of—the wisdom of the first, whereas Harry, the unlikeable character who vies with him for leadership, advocates the second. In the end Ben, whose perspective the film supports, is proven wrong; he survives by taking refuge in the cellar after the others have been killed.

The futility of rational discourse is demonstrated in the final sequence when the sheriff's shambling posse converges on the zombie-beseiged farmhouse. The newsman at the scene comments, "everything appears to be under control," the forces of law and order are on hand to destroy the "marauding ghouls." It is at this point that the (white) posse kills the night's sole (black) survivor, Ben, mistaking him for a zombie. The implication is that this mistake was not an isolated incident and that chaos now reigns in a more familiar form. In fact, shortly before they come to the farmhouse, Sheriff McClellan tells the newsman that they killed three zombies "trying to claw their way into an abandoned shed. They must have thought somebody was in there. There wasn't though."

No doubt the sheriff would describe the farmhouse as abandoned. Ben's body is dragged out on a baling hook to be burned on a bonfire in the company of the zombies he successfully fought off.

It is much remarked upon by critics that in this 1968 film no character remarks upon the hero's race. This silence is particularly noticeable when Harry, a narrow-minded character, describes him as a "man" rather than as a "black man." This racial silence is the structuring absence that resounds in the concluding sequence of the film. The grainy black-and-white still-action sequence in which white men dump dead bodies onto a bonfire, here a literalized version of the bone-fire, suggests both the violence of white supremacists like the Ku Klux Klan and television's contemporaneous routine presentation of the bloodshed in Vietnam.

At the conclusion of the film, the small group is dead and the onslaught continues. The forces of law and order take on the function of marauders, killing indiscriminately, virtually indistinguishable from the zombies. The rampage is epidemic in scope, its character virtually unstoppable, and humanity's prospects for survival bleak. (Indeed, Romero's sequels *Dawn of the Dead* [1979] and *Day of the Dead* [1985] are equally bleak.) The world of reason is annihilated. The effect is that of pulling the rug out from under the feet of the viewer. We can only be secure in the knowledge that there is no security. Postmodern horror confronts us with the necessity for an epistemology of uncertainty: we only know that we do not know.

Postmodern Horror Repudiates Narrative Closure

The classical horror film constructs a secure universe characterized by narrative closure, one in which (hu)man agency (human agency understood as male agency) prevails and the normative order is restored by film's end.[11] In contrast, violating narrative closure has become de rigueur for the postmodern genre. The film may come to an end, but it is an open ending. Before turning to this, I will for purposes of comparison briefly look at the form of narrative resolution that the postmodern genre refuses, a resolution prevalent in the classical horror film: The monster is destroyed and the normative order restored.

In the classical horror film, the monster is an irrational Other who precipitates violence and transgresses the law. It is evil because it threatens the social order; the suppression of the unleashed menace is a priority for the agents of order. The violence of the law restores repression, and the social order is reestablished. This is the ending that best conforms to the status quo and regards departures from it as chaotic and evil. In *The Thing* (1951), the alien creature threatens to transform the human race into livestock until it is destroyed by the military. Through military might, the world is kept safe for (anticommunist) democracy, and the clarion call for vigilance against further threats is rung.

Although the postmodern genre typically repudiates narrative closure, it is instructive to look at an exception to this—a self-reflexive 1988 film characterized by narrative closure. *The Lady in White* is a look back at the classical horror film that is nonetheless marked by the postmodern paradigm. It is a ghost story set in 1962 about a nine-year-old boy named Frankie who writes monster stories (at least one of which is open-ended) and who collects monster figures: Frankenstein, Dracula, and the Wolfman. Frankie embarks on a two-fold search to uncover the identity of a psychotic who is molesting and killing children (and who nearly kills him), and to reunite the first victim, Melissa, with the ghost of her mother, the lady in white. As befits the postmodern paradigm, the film blurs the boundary between normal and abnormal, so that the killer is revealed to be Phil, the surrogate brother of Frankie's father Angelo.

Phil, a likeable family member, orphaned as a boy and raised by Angelo's parents, is someone the boy trusts. Moreover, it is ordinary people, Frankie and his brother Geno, who investigate and fight the psychotic. Inept police authorities arrest the wrong man. But in a departure from the postmodern genre, the film is set in the past, persistently shuns body horror, and ties up all the loose ends: Frankie is saved (by the lady in white, her sister, and his father), the ghosts of mother and daughter are reunited, and the killer dies in an act of expiation. The film is indeed a nostalgic look at what John McCarty (1990, 228) calls, "the kinder, gentler days of horror," B.C. (Before Carnage).[12]

The Lady in White is a good illustration of how the features under discussion apply to the majority of contemporary horror films, though not necessarily to all. Narrative closure is a *dominant* feature of the classical, but a *residual* feature of the postmodern genre. Similarly, open-ended narratives are dominant in the postmodern, but *emergent* in the classical genre, as I will show in my discussion of *Invaders from Mars* (1953).[13]

In the postmodern horror film either the monster triumphs or the outcome is uncertain.

The Monster Triumphs

The monster precipitates violence and transgresses the law. Neither is the monster unambiguously evil nor the social order unambiguously good. The monster is the "return of the repressed," which overturns a highly flawed social order (Wood 1978). This ending throws into question the immutability and desirability of the status quo (Wood 1983). In *They Came From Within* (1976), a worm-like parasite that unleashes people's sexual inhibitions runs amok in an emotionally sterile, middle-class housing complex. The result is a violent breakdown of sexual taboos: promiscuity, intergenerational sex, incest [all heterosexual], and lesbianism. The excess of released desires is predetermined by the surplus repression to which they were subjected by the puritanical impulses of bourgeois society. In the end, the infected become normative in the housing complex, and the inhabitants drive off, presumably to venereally infect the larger population.

The Outcome Is Uncertain

Although in the end the monster appears to be vanquished, the film concludes with signs of a new unleashing; the apparent triumph over the monster is temporary at best. Evil prevails as the monster continues to disrupt the normative order. In *Dressed to Kill* (1980), Brian De Palma reprises the ending of *Carrie* (1976). The psychopath who murders women that threaten his transsexual designs is ostensibly thwarted when he is injured and apprehended. However, the complacency with which the film threatens to close is disrupted by the final violent sequence in which the killer escapes from a mental hospital, breaks into the house that Liz, the protagonist, is staying in, and slashes her throat. Though we learn that this sequence is a nightmare when she wakes up screaming, clutching her intact throat, the transition is so abrupt that it leaves us shaken and uncertain, nowhere near closure.

This highly ambiguous form of the open ending in which danger and disruption are endemic prevails. Narratives are apt to end apocalyptically with the defeat of the protagonists or with incipient signs of a new unleashing.[14] This rule applies even to *Alien*, which ostensibly provides narrative closure, since the creature is catapulted into the void of space. However, the film ends with all but one of the original eggs intact on the planet's surface. Thus, even within the parameters of the closed narrative, the potential for a continuation of the threat is implicit.

Just as some postmodern horror films retain some characteristics of the classical genre, so too, some classical films, such as *Invaders from Mars* (1953), in their pessimism and undecidability were forerunners of the postmodern horror film. Early in *Invaders from Mars*, twelve-year-old David is awakened by a violent electrical storm. When he gets up to close the window, he witnesses the landing of a flying saucer in an adjoining sand pit. David's parents reassure him that it was just a dream, but his father George, a rocket scientist, decides to investigate. When he approaches the sand he is sucked down and vanishes. He returns a changed man, hostile and bearing a scar on the back of his neck. Police officers who subsequently investigate the field are similarly transformed. David's attempts to warn people are dismissed as the products of an overactive imagination. Unable to marshal the community, David turns to Professor Kelston, an astronomer who calls in Colonel Fielding, a benevolent military man who knows how to defeat the Martians. It is David's hope that when the Martians are destroyed, those enslaved, including his parents, will be restored to their former selves.

Had the film ended here, it would have been a typical horror film of the classical era. The collective monster emanates from an exotic location. The Martians are unequivocably evil. People are unequivocably good, that is, until they are abducted and enslaved through a brain implant which compels them to act on behalf of the Martians. The enslaved humans are perceptibly altered in their demeanor; they are cold and harsh. Heroic scientific and military experts would have conquered the monster and the benevolent normative order would have been reinstated. But that is *not* how it ends. As the Martian spacecraft explodes, David awakens from a nightmare. Moments later, thunder booms and he leaps to the window to see the saucer land in the sand pit. Either David is awakening from a dream to find that the events of his nightmare are coming true, Martians are invading, or he is caught within a viciously repetitive nightmare from which he cannot awaken, à la *Nightmare on Elm Street*. We are left with this open ending, unable to determine where the nightmare begins or ends, or whether it ends at all.[15] The film's dream structure blurs the distinction between objective and subjective representation.

Similarly, the framing narrative of *Dead of Night* (1945), an English anthology film, fits the postmodern paradigm. An architect arrives for a weekend at a farmhouse he has been commissioned to redesign. There he meets the assembled guests and experiences a strong sense of déjà vu. He believes he has lived through this experience in a dream. To convince the others, he volunteers recollected fragments of events to come. One of the guests, a psychiatrist tries to explain away this evidence. The others are more sympathetic. Several of them proceed to tell bizarre tales, each of which constitutes a separate segment of the film. At the end, the architect recalls that in his dream he is inexplicably compelled to murder the psychiatrist. After he kills the doctor he flees through the settings of the stories earlier recounted until he is killed. Then the phone rings and he awakens from a nightmare that he cannot recall. It is a client inviting him out to a farmhouse . . . At the end, the horror begins all over again in both films.

Two Tell-Tale *Things*

The shift from classical to postmodern paradigms is well illustrated by comparing the 1951 and 1982 versions of *The Thing*. In the 1951 version a flying saucer crashes near an American scientific installation at the North Pole. A military team under the leadership of Captain Pat Hendry is called in to investigate. They inadvertently destroy the ship but are able to retrieve an alien encased in a block of ice. The distinction between alien and human is unmistakeably drawn by its physical appearance and demeanor. The Thing is hairless, with "crazy" eyes and hands. Moreover, the creature is indelibly marked as alien by its inability or unwillingness to speak and its lack of emotion. In contrast, the military men engage in friendly banter and sustain their good spirits throughout the crisis.

When the ice thaws the Thing escapes, though not before losing a hand and forearm in a scuffle with the sled dogs. The bloodless severed limb contains the plant-based creature's reproductive seeds. Dr. Carrington, a Nobelist and leader of the scientific team, in violation of military orders sets up a nursery in which to cultivate the seeds with the needed blood. Most of the scientists concur with the military that the Thing is an "unpredictably dangerous" invader that must be annihilated before it can grow its own army. But Carrington steadfastly refuses to listen, insisting that "there can be no enemies in science." At the suggestion of Nikki, Carrington's secretary and Pat's romantic interest, the men decide to "cook" it by setting it on fire. When that fails they try again with unquenched optimism. This time they try electrocution. In a misguided effort to further science, Carrington sabotages their plan by turning off the generator. When he attempts to communicate with the creature it responds with a buffeting blow. With Carrington out of the way, the military men obliterate the alien. Thanks to the efficacy of military experts who band together in a well-coordinated effort to defeat the monster, the world is safe. In a final touch of narrative closure, Pat and Nikki banter about marriage.

This film is structured around the act of telling. The violence is offscreen or shadowed and bloodless. The enemy is readily identifiable and vulnerable to the efforts of the (predominantly male) cooperative community. The ending warns of the possibility of future invasions, as the reporter cautions, "watch the skies." But the admonition is couched in the confident belief, which characters hold throughout the film, that (hu)man agency will prevail.

The 1982 remake, credited as "John Carpenter's *The Thing*," employs the same Thing logo as its predecessor but constructs a profoundly different narrative.[16] The film opens in Antarctica with a Norwegian helicopter in deadly pursuit of a sled dog. The animal reaches an American science station where it takes refuge among the men. In the hunt, one Norwegian inadvertently blows himself up. After missing the dog and wounding one of the Americans, the other is shot dead by the camp commander, Garry. MacReady (Kurt Russell) pilots Doc Cooper to the Norwegian camp to seek out an explanation for such irrational behavior. They find the incinerated shell of the camp, the remains of a bloodbath, a partially thawed block of ice, records, and a monstrous carcass. They hurriedly transport the carcass and camp records back to base before the brunt of a storm hits. The videotape they recover shows the Norwegians forming a human circle around the ice-immersed spacecraft and retrieving the alien in a block of ice. In a sense, the Norwegians play out the story line of the earlier *Thing* except that they fail to survive.

Blair's autopsy of the carcass—two faces in a rictus of torture, terror, or rage melding together into a morass of body parts—reveals that though the outward appearance is freakish, the internal organs are normal. The scientist concludes that this is an organism that can imitate other life forms. Given enough time, the copy is virtually indistinguishable from the real thing. In the paranoid world of postmodern horror, the monster effectively "passes,"[17] first as a dog then as human, infiltrating and breeding suspicion among the ranks. The first to be named a suspect is Clark, the one who tends the dogs, due to his lengthy proximity to the dog-thing. When the dog-thing attacks the dogs in the kennel it reveals one of its multiple alien forms as orifices, tentacles, and secretions erupt from its increasingly unrecognizable body. Although the Thing reveals various alien forms throughout the film, it is unclear if any of these is its "real" or original form. They may simply be forms of prior conquests. The Thing is the ultimate simulacra, constantly generating copies without originals.[18]

The bodily transformation scenes are staged as attacks by the Thing on people or animals. As such, the appearance of the Thing in its monstrous guise signals the onset of a violent attack on the normal body that will render it a ruined body. The metamorphosis scenes serve not to reassure us with information about the underlying "face" of the monster, what the monster *really* looks like, but to horrify us with the bloody, viscous, and unpredictable transformations of the monster's body and the body of its victim. Appendages and orifices sprout from unforeseeable sources in uncanny combinations. Any*body* can be harboring this secret.

The film throws into question the distinction between reality and appearance, human and alien, by contrasting the apparent normality of the crew with the knowledge that some are not human. Since only a particle of the alien is sufficient to attack, the men dispense with communal dining and each one prepares canned meals for himself. What was a fragmented community from the outset of the film disintegrates rapidly into a group torn by mutual mistrust and bickering. Blair, the scientist, cracks under the weight of impending doom and is placed in isolation. Shortly before they are to conduct a blood-based experiment to determine who is human and who is not, the blood bank is drained. The next to be named as suspects are those with access to the blood. This includes Garry who must rescind his command. MacReady assumes the mantle of leadership, but he foresees defeat. He makes a tape to tell the tale in the event that no one survives. His pessimism is warranted.

The group's primary problem is how to identify the enemy when the Thing metamorphoses into a perfect simulacrum of its victim. As such, the 1982 *Thing* can be considered a post-Vietnam film, stamped by the American soldier's inability to distinguish between friend or foe, the war's futile loss of life, and their eventual defeat. The Thing takes on the appearance and personality of the crew members it kills, becoming a multiple and indeterminate monster. To exacerbate matters, the Thing plants misleading clues about the identity of the monster; it effectively throws suspicion on MacReady, the character best equipped to organize the struggle against it. Mac is left outside to die but uses force to retake control.

During the altercation, Norris goes into cardiac arrest. When the doctor applies electric defibrillator pads to resuscitate him, his chest erupts in a cavernous maw and cleaves the doctor's arms off. As the men bombard it with flame throwers the Norris-thing's head detaches from the burning body, sprouts spider-like legs and scuttles off. This gives Mac an idea. He has them tie each other up and introduces a test. He reasons that since each particle of the monster can exist independently of the rest, when intense heat is applied to a blood sample drawn from a Thing, the blood will self-protectively flee, much as the head did. (As he conducts the invader-identifying blood test, we see behind him an old venereal disease poster proclaiming "They aren't labeled, chum.") One by one he tests the men who are noticeably terrified of the outcome, as though they fear they might be monsters and not know it, as if the men did not know they were replicas but were about to find out. They breathe a deep sigh of relief when they pass the test and regain their freedom. Garry insistently regards the test with disbelief until Palmer proves its validity. Throughout the film the human crew members suspect and even kill each other, but they never suspect a "thing" until it is too late, as the latter scene demonstrates. Mac's test, though effective, is ill-thought out. When the Palmer-thing erupts, Garry and Childs are bound next to it unable to escape. Mac's flamethrower jams. Windows is frozen with fear and fails to fire. By the time Mac is able to fire, Windows is dead.

Garry and Childs, the two remaining prisoners, pass the test. It is at this point that they remember Blair has been sequestered in the toolshed for much of the crisis. Blair is, of course, a Thing and has utilized this opportunity to build a spaceship. The Thing always seems to be one step ahead of them, a fact that lends a note of pessimism to the ending. The Thing blows up the generator to freeze the base. People will die, but the cold will preserve it until a rescue party arrives in the Spring. Mac decides to dynamite the station hoping to kill it. As they fully realize, this move will destroy them too. Thus they deprive the Thing of host or haven, a chemotherapy of sorts in which some die so that the social body might have a chance to survive. At the end, Mac and Childs share a bottle of booze as they prepare to freeze to death. The final shot shows the camp burning to the ground, progressively losing form, engulfed by snow banks, much like the Norwegian camp.

As Stephen Prince's (1988) structuralist comparison points out, the destruction of the station leads to formlessness; the landscape becomes structureless as all boundaries are eradicated. Whether this undifferentiated mass indicates the destruction of the monster, the elimination of matter out of place, or the triumph of a monster with no apparent necessary form is indeterminate. At the conclusion of the film, we do not know if the virtually indestructible monster has been destroyed; the men will surely die, and the fate of humanity hangs in the balance. Such is the pessimism of the postmodern horror film. What makes it tolerable for the monster to persist in the open-ended narrative is the genre's construction of recreational terror.

Horror Produces a Bounded Experience of Fear

> Behind the lights faces watch from the darkness
> ready to laugh or scream in terror.
>
> —*New Nightmare* (1994)

Horror is an exercise in recreational terror, a simulation of danger not unlike a roller coaster ride. Like the latter, people in a confined space are kept off-balance through the use of suspense and precipitous surprises achieved by alternating between seeing what lies ahead and being in the dark (for instance, tunnels and other shadowy regions, closed or shielded eyes). Throughout, the element of control, the conviction that there is nothing to be afraid of turns stress/arousal (beating heart, dry mouth, panic grip) into a pleasurable sensation. Fear and pleasure commingle. Indeed, the physical and emotional thrills experienced by a horror audience may be akin to the biochemical reactions stimulated by the intense physical excitement of a roller-coaster ride. This relation is suggested by the etymology of "horror" as traced by Carroll (1990, 24), who claims that the word derives from Latin and Old French terms which mean "to bristle" as in the current use of "horripilate."

The horror film is an exquisite exercise in coping with the terrors of everyday life. Earlier I argued that the horror film violates everyday life. This is true on the narrative level, but on the level of unconscious operations, it is more accurate to say that horror exposes the terror *implicit* in everyday life: the pain of loss, the enigma of death, the unpredictability of events, the inadequacy of intentions. It seems odd to talk about everyday life in terms of terror precisely because terror is a routinely repressed aspect of everyday life. According to Henri Lefebvre in *Everyday Life in the Modern World*, the repression of terror is incessant and ubiquitous; repression operates "at all levels, at all times and in every sphere of experience" (1984, 145). Ironically, repression is effective precisely because everyday life seems spontaneous and "natural" and, therefore, exempt from repression.

Horror denaturalizes the repressed by transmuting the "natural" elements of everyday life into the unnatural form of the monster. In *Night of the Living Dead*, the mindless malevolence of a racist society (here and in Southeast Asia) is transmuted into the rampage of a group of zombies. This transmutation renders the terrors of everyday life at least emotionally accessible. By monstrifying quotidian terrors, horror unearths the repressed. This process is similar to the dream work described by Freud (1966). Much as dreams displace and condense repressed thoughts and feelings, so horror films introduce monstrous elements to disguise the quotidian terrors of everyday life. Much as dreams are unconscious attempts to express conflicts and resolve tensions, so horror films allow the audience to express and thus, to some extent, master feelings too threatening to articulate consciously.[19] The horror film is the equivalent of the cultural nightmare, processing material that is simultaneously attractive and repellent, displayed and obfuscated, desired and repressed. Just as Freud regards dreams, even distressing ones, as wish fulfillments of repressed desires, so I regard the horror film as an amalgam of desire and inhibition, fascination and fear.

Just as a dream must process repressed material so that the dreamer does not wake up, recreational terror must produce a bounded experience that will not generate so much distress that the seasoned horror audience member will walk out. In order to produce recreational terror, the re-creation of terror must be only partial. As Michael Taussig defines it, terror is the threat to the body and the concomitant sense that harm could happen to you. Taussig (1989, 13–15) likens the reign of terror in Colombia to a "Hobbesian world, nasty, brutish, and short, in which . . . 'you can't trust anyone'"—a world in which paranoia prevails and "dream and reality commingle," in other words, a world much like the fictional universe of postmodern horror.

In terror, there is no insulation and no recreation because the re-creation of danger is complete, whereas in recreational terror, the violation and death of the body is experienced as partial. The experience of terror is bounded by the tension between proximity and distance, reality and illusion. In recreational terror, we fear the threat of physical danger, but the danger fails to materialize. *Targets* self-reflexively narrativizes the violation of this parameter when the psychotic killer snipes at the drive-in audience watching *The Terror*, thus converting the fantasized threat of physical danger into reality. This self-reflexive turn becomes particularly acute if we consider that the film was probably on the drive-in circuit. Earlier (*The Blob* [1958]) and more recent films (*Demons* [1985], *Anguish* [1988], and *Popcorn* [1991]) also employ the twist of having the audience of a horror film attacked in the theater. (Some recent entries recognize that much horror film viewing takes place at home as television screenings, for instance *Demons 2: The Nightmare Returns* [1986].) Recreational terror can rehearse the threat of physical harm to the fictional moviegoer precisely because, if not impossible, it is highly unlikely to happen in the movie theater (or at home as a result of watching television). Having successfully undergone the ordeal, we experience a sense of relief and mastery, proportionate to the intensity of the ordeal.

Much as the horror film is an exercise in terror, it is simultaneously an exercise in mastery, in which controlled loss substitutes for loss of control. It allows us to give free rein to culturally repressed feelings such as terror and rage. It constructs situations where these taboo feelings are sanctioned. This bounded experience of terror is constructed through various means: the temporally and spatially finite nature of film, the semipublic setting of film exhibition, the acquisition of insider knowledge, and the use of comedy. I will look at each in turn as it applies to the horror film.

The Temporally and Spatially Finite Nature of Film

A film promises a contained experience. What makes it tolerable for the monster to persist in the open ending is the containment of the menace within the temporal and spatial frame of the film. Film viewers learn from experience that the average running time of a feature film is about 90 minutes. Consequently, regardless of how open an ending may be, the film ends, and in this there is a modicum of closure. In *Dressed to Kill*, the tidying up of loose ends occurs nearly an hour into the film. Its temporal location marks it as a false ending. The actual ending comes abruptly on the heels of a profoundly threatening scene from which the audience is not given time to recover. In contrast, the false ending in *Alien* comes at a point marked as an appropriate place for an ending: over 90 minutes have elapsed, the spaceship—and presumably its alien passenger—is destroyed, and the hero, Ripley, is hurtling through space preparing for the voyage home. She is behaving as though she were alone, stripped down to her underwear, vulnerable. The shot of the alien inside the shuttle craft comes as a shock to the audience, as it does to Ripley. The film concludes shortly thereafter, with the expulsion (and presumed destruction) of the alien.

A film is not only a time-bound experience, it is also an imaginary one. The screen constitutes the spatial frame on which a film is projected. It marks off a bounded reality, one that need not conform strictly to lived experience. The borders of the screen establish parameters that free the viewer to engage in fantasy. The borders of the movie theater constitute film viewing as a semipublic activity.

The Semipublic Setting of Film Exhibition

A movie theater is a semipublic setting, both communal and solitary. It is accessible to the public, for a price, and designed to seat a group in a common space. But it is also a solitary setting: a darkened arena, where the film projector throws a pool of light at the screen, which becomes the collective visual focal point. It is a setting in which people tacitly agree to ignore each other during the course of the film. At the same time, the juxtaposition of public and private dimensions generates a space for legitimate social interaction among audience members. The degree of legitimate public response varies by community of audience. For instance, the experience of watching *Aliens* (1986) in the Times Square vicinity with a boisterous audience was for me very different and far more pleasurable than seeing it in East Hampton, where the audience was subdued, to say the least. The Times Square audience, a racially and economically mixed group, unabashedly let out loud screams, laughter, gasps, sarcastic remarks and exclamations. They issued warnings to characters or predicted their demise. In contrast, the more affluent and white East Hampton audience quietly murmured to their viewing companions and barely let out a scream.

These two contemporaneous movie theater audiences parallel what historian Lawrence Levine describes in *Highbrow/Lowbrow: The Emergence of Cultural Hierarchy in America* as the raucous audience and the passive audience. Levine chronicles the process by which the unruly audiences of the eighteenth and nineteenth centuries were disciplined into the docile audiences of today. By the twentieth century, "audiences in America had become less interactive, less of a public and more of a group of mute receptors" (1988, 195). Levine also mentions that the behavior of audiences for popular entertainment changed significantly but not completely, and names sports and religious audiences as exceptions to the docile norm. I would include most, though not all, horror audiences in the exceptions, as my experience with *Aliens* demonstrates.

Watching a horror film is, like riding a roller coaster, a collective experience. Horror expressly plays on the physical and emotional responses of the audience. It elicits screams, nervous gasps, and laughter. When an involuntary scream escapes our lips, it is reassuring to hear it echoed in the screams of others—followed by embarrassed titters. Horror elicits audience rebukes and warnings addressed *to* narrative characters ("Don't go in there"), or *about* narrative characters ("Heeeeere's Jason"). A Gary Larson cartoon captures this dynamic to a tee: A group of deer is watching a film in which a deer character approaches a door over which hangs a mounted deer trophy. The audience cringes, and one member cries out, "Don't go in there!"

Such remarks serve several functions:

1. On the simplest level, they evoke the tension-breaking laughter that steers us away from being terrorized.
2. They constitute attempts to master the situation by taking an authoritative stance; the speaker indicates that s/he would *never* be so foolish as to do that.
3. As Tudor (1989, 112) points out, the competent audience member knows that the warning is futile but nevertheless issues it to express her or his own ambivalence about the dangers of risk-taking. This entails a splitting of the ambivalence, whereby the narrative character performs the dangerous activity while the audience member remains secure, yet vicariously enjoys the danger.
4. The collective response serves as a reminder that "you are not alone," "it's only a movie," and thus serves to reanchor the viewer near the shores of reality.

5. These remarks serve as forms of interaction with other members of the audience, who monitor each other's responses and react to them in turn, with laughter or remarks of their own.

Thus, the collective response facilitates the construction of the audience, a heterogeneous group with simultaneous but diverse responses that shares the parameters of the genre but within those parameters variety operates freely. The interactive character of the horror audience is recognized by the film industry, which will sometimes exhort audience participation through the use of gimmickry like "Percepto": through the installation of devices under theater seats, audience members received mild electric shocks to incite them to scream during screenings of *The Tingler* (1959).[20] Other gimmicks include giving away "barf bags" for *I Dismember Mama* (1974) or vampire dentures for *Dracula Has Risen from the Grave* (1968). The audience shares not only the experience of the moment, but also a past; it is an audience with a history of viewing.

The Acquisition of Insider Knowledge

Repeated exposure to horror fiction constitutes a process of socialization that seasons the audience member. The competent audience acquires knowledge that conditions expectations about the genre. The genre, in turn, arouses, disappoints, and redirects these expectations. Innovations within instances of the genre, before they attain the status of cliché, ensure that the seasoning process is never complete. Even the most weathered audience is vulnerable to the possibility of innovation, to a shocking combination of elements that violates expectations based on preceding instances of the genre. The seasoned audience is familiar with narrative motifs and character types, with camera work and musical codes that warn of impending violence. When the adolescent rational skeptic wanders off into the woods of Crystal Lake (the preferred setting for *Friday the 13th* films), and the music takes on an ominous tone, can violence be far behind? Narrative pleasure derives from the intelligibility of the genre, from appreciating the deployment of generic conventions to discern the logic to the madness and from innovations that violate audience expectations.

Insider knowledge is especially high in serial films such as *Halloween*, *Friday the 13th*, and *A Nightmare on Elm Street*. The serial audience shares the pleasure of privileged information about Michael, Jason, and Freddy, the respective killers in these films.[21] As members of a competent audience, we can bask in the knowledge that *we* would not act as foolishly as the killer's victims; *we* would know what to do. Insider knowledge provides a measure of security. If we understand it, if we have some idea of what to expect, it becomes less menacing and we can brave it. In *Aliens*, when the search party nears the nest, those in the audience who have seen *Alien* know the soldiers are perilously close, but they are unaware of the danger. Even Ripley, the narrative link between the two films, does not know; she was not a member of the search party in the original film. This is the privileged position of the sequel audience.

The self-reflexive *New Nightmare* (1994) stages a story in which a competent audience member "Heather Langenkamp" (played by Heather Langenkamp who played Nancy in the first and third *Nightmare on Elm Street* films) is thrust into a postmodern universe in which the fictional Freddy Krueger makes deadly incursions into the realm of the "real."[22] As "Wes Craven" (played by Wes Craven, the director and writer of the original film and this one) puts it, "He's decided to cross over, out of films into our reality." Freddy kills Heather's husband and other members of the special-effects crew working on the new *Nightmare* movie which Wes is directing. As Wes explains, because Heather is the gatekeeper in his dreams, which he claims inspired the two *Nightmare* scripts, Freddy must get past Heather if he is to enter the real. So he is attacking those she holds dearest including her young son Dylan whom Freddy abducts. To stop him Heather must reprise her role as Nancy "one last time" and engage him in battle. The film ends with Freddy's fiery destruction in a nightmare shared by Heather and Dylan, and the latter duo's return to reality. At the foot of the bed lies a script. When Heather turns to the last page we see a description of the scene that has been unfolding. Dylan asks her to read him the story. She turns to the beginning and reads a description of the opening scene. "Behind the lights faces watch from the darkness ready to laugh or scream in terror . . ."

The Use of Comedy

As this line suggests, comedy and terror are closely tied in recreational terror. Comedy serves a double, paradoxical function in horror films; it creates both distance and proximity. Most notably, it produces the proverbial comic relief, the cessation of terror, thus providing the requisite *distance* to stave off terrorism at strategic points. The comic turn is expressed in horror film titles such as *Chopping Mall* (1986) or *I Dismember Mama*, and by several characters. Freddy Krueger flaunts his razor wit in *A Nightmare on Elm Street 3: Dream Warriors* (1987) when he derides a mute boy, calling him tongue-tied, then proceeds to suspend him over a pit, his wrists and ankles tied with tongues.

Humor frequently involves self-reflexive references to other horror films. In a direct allusion to insider knowledge about slasher films, an endangered character in *Friday the 13th Part VI: Jason Lives* (1986) exclaims, "I've seen enough horror films to know this means trouble." Playing on older audience members' knowledge about horror films, characters in *The Howling*, a film about New Age werewolves, watch the 1941 version of *The Wolf Man*. In addition, characters in *The Howling* are named after directors of other werewolf films: George Waggner (*The Wolf Man*) and Terry Fisher (*The Curse of the Werewolf* [1960]). It includes among the cast Kevin McCarthy (who played the lead in *Invasion of the Body Snatchers* [1956]); Forrest Ackerman, former editor of *Famous Monsters of Filmland*; and director/producer Roger Corman.

Playing on more contemporary audience members' knowledge, *Hello Mary Lou: Prom Night II*'s (1987) intertextual references cannibalize *Carrie* and *The Exorcist*. In this film, Mary Lou is about to be crowned prom queen when a nasty prank by her jilted boyfriend turns deadly and she burns to death (à la *Carrie*). Thirty years later her spirit possesses Vicki, a candidate for prom queen whose mother is obsessed with religion. In a direct reference to *The Exorcist*, Vicki's personality change is described as "Linda Blairsville" by one of the characters, the words "help me" appear on a malevolent blackboard, and a priest attempts to perform an exorcism (chanting "the body of Christ compels you").

Fredric Jameson refers to the cannibalization of past productions as pastiche, an ironic self-awareness that calls attention to its own constructedness. Pastiche, the art of plagiarism, is the postmodern code that supplants modernism's unique mark of style (1991, 16). I am disturbed by the characterization, stated or implied, of pastiche as exclusively a postmodern phenomenon. When it comes to the horror film, pastiche is a long-standing practice. The film cycles of the thirties and forties abound in countless remakes and sequels, although not enumerated as they are today.[23] Pastiche is not a new theme; however, in the contemporary genre there has been an intensification.[24]

The primary difference between contemporary pastiche and that of earlier decades is the prominence of graphic violence to produce gory humor, what McCarty (1984) calls "splatstick," a cross between splatter (his term for gore) and slapstick. A good example of a film in which the comic turn overtakes the horror is *Evil Dead II* (1987). When the hero, Ash, is bitten on the hand by a zombie, the hand becomes possessed and proceeds to assault him. In self-defense, Ash amputates the malevolent member which continues to be animate. Ash's inspired, though ineffectual, solution is to confine the hand in a container weighted down by a stack of books with *A Farewell to Arms* on top, an over-the-top touch.[25]

Comedy in horror operates in a second way. It produces incongruous, contradictory, or illogical effects that create *proximity* to the terror at hand. Since both comedy and horror depend on what David Bordwell and Kristin Thompson (1979, 31) call "the radical cheating of expectations," one can be used to produce the other. The horror genre must keep terror and comedy in tension if it is to successfully tread the thin line that separates it from terrorism and parody. If terror produces an excess of proximity, the result is terrorism. If comedy produces an excess of distance, the result is parody.[26] In "Horrality—The Textuality of Contemporary Horror Films," Brophy treats humor as a constituent feature of postmodern horror and characterizes it as "mostly perverse and/or tasteless, so much so that often the humour might be horrific while the horror might be humorous" (1986, 13).[27]

This delicate balance is struck in *The Texas Chain Saw Massacre* in which the decaying, yet marginally animate, corpse of Grandpa not only incorporates horrific and humorous effects but actually utilizes one to exacerbate the other. The humor is born of the absurdity of storing the mummified corpses of Grandpa, Grandma, and the family dog, figures of domesticity, in an upstairs chamber. The "boys" have trouble bringing the patriarchal mummy downstairs. They revive him by letting him suck the blood from Sally's lacerated finger. The ancient patriarch of this family of displaced slaughterhouse workers is simultaneously a totemic figure who represents the romanticized past when manual slaughter prevailed in the butcher industry, and a bald, wrinkled, infantile dependent whose limbs quiver like a baby's when he suck(le)s blood. The horror is born of the torment of the young woman subjected to imprisonment and abuse amidst decaying human arms (she is tied to the "arm chair") and mobiles made of human bones and teeth. In this horrific context, "Sally's screams become less emotive than inevitable, a wall paper of sound where laughter is no less appropriate than fear" (Davies 1996, 4). She is caught in a bedlam where the madmen are free and the others are destroyed or driven to insanity. In bewilderment, we cringe at the gallows humor and laugh at the terror.

The *Texas Chain Saw Massacre* is an exemplary instance of the postmodern horror genre that constructs an unstable, open-ended universe in which categories collapse, violence constitutes everyday life, and the irrational prevails. The proliferation of apocalyptic, graphically violent films that dot the post-sixties landscape attest to the need to express rage and terror in the midst of postmodern social upheaval. The genre constructs the occasion for recreational terror in which con-

FIGURE 1.2. The postmodern horror film uses comedy and horror in tandem to make us cringe at the gallows humor and laugh at the terror. In *The Texas Chain Saw Massacre* (1974), Sally is tied to an "arm chair." Courtesy of Museum of Modern Art Film Stills Archive.

trolled loss substitutes for loss of control. The experience is as much an exercise in mastery as it is an exercise in terror. We are not, after all, overcome by the monster. If the image becomes too much to bear, we can avert our eyes. It is a test of our mettle to survive the ordeal, and yet the ordeal itself is not without its pleasures. It is a welcome release from the fiction that life is ordered and safe. Horror affords us the opportunity to express our fear of living in a minefield, or perhaps more accurately, it affords us the opportunity, to borrow Annette Kolodny's (1980) phrase, to dance through the minefield.

CHAPTER TWO

The Pleasure of Seeing/Not-Seeing the Spectacle of the Wet Death

Unlike classical horror films, which tell and imply but show very little of the destruction wrought upon the human body, the postmodern horror film is obsessed with the wet death, intent on imaging the mutilation and destruction of the body. The genre's fascination with the spectacle of the ruined body necessitates its privileging of the act of showing (Brophy 1986, 8). But the act of showing the ruined body is only half the story; the other half is the act of concealing, of producing a partial vision. The dialectic between seeing and not-seeing is so crucial to the production of recreational terror that it operates not only at the level of the film but also at the level of the audience and at the institutional intersection between the two known as the special-effects magazine.

The Pleasure of Not-seeing

Easily overlooked in many discussions of the spectacle of horror is the degree to which not being able to see structures the act of looking. Dennis Giles refers to the recreational terror produced by a "delayed, blocked or partial vision" as "the pleasure in *not-seeing*" (1984, 41). A partial vision negotiates the tension between the desire to see and dread at the prospect of seeing. The tension between seeing and not-seeing operates in the *solitary reaction shot* and the *unclaimed point-of-view*

(POV) shot, a battery of distinctive shots that signify the monster's presence. In the solitary reaction shot we see the victim's terrified reaction—a terror-stricken face frozen in a scream—but the monster's body is largely withheld from sight, leaving the viewer wondering what the monster looks like and what it is doing to the victim. As J. P. Telotte (1980, 146–47) points out, what is unsettling about this convention is that it subverts rationality by reversing cause and effect. We see the effect (the incredulous stare of the victim) without seeing the cause (the monster).

In the unclaimed POV shot, one or a series of shots is held long enough and framed in order to create the impression that someone is watching, but without a reverse shot to show us who.[1] The unclaimed POV shot condenses three looks: the look of the camera, the look of the spectator, and the implied look of the monster. Several variants of this disembodied look are common. First is a tracking shot that keeps most or all of the monster's body out of the frame but provides an acoustic close-up of the monster's heavy breathing. The stalking sequence at the end of *Dressed to Kill* offers one example of this disembodied look. Second is a tracking shot that allows us to see some part of the monster's body from the monster's point of view but refrains from revealing the identity of the killer. The opening of *Halloween* is a five-minute sequence done in this fashion. Third is a series of voyeuristic shots, either tracking or stationary, taken from assorted angles and points in the narrative space, and placed behind a window, doorway, or other framing device to create the keyhole effect of surveillance by an unseen or partially seen other. The haphazard character of this movement between unconnected points in narrative space defies linear logic and produces a vague, menacing presence by withholding a lucid picture of the threat.

The unclaimed POV shot operates in tandem with the solitary reaction shot to obscure the image and identity of the monster while simultaneously showing the spectacle of the terrorized and ravaged victim. The inability to see what is not shown heightens the power of the image to horrify.

Like framing, lighting works to hide as much as it exposes. The chiaroscuro tradition of lighting in the horror film uses the play of light and darkness to invoke "an unknown and unseen presence" (Neale 1980, 43). Similarly, Telotte alludes to the pleasure of not-seeing when he argues that the horror film is most effective when "dark patches and vague presences" feed our desire to conjure up monsters (1990, 153).[2] The prominence of blind space in the horror film, what lurks outside the frame or unclearly within it, generates uncertainty about what one is seeing. Carroll observes that through such elements as editing, camera angle, lighting, and set design, the horror film problematizes the clarity and duration of the image in order to throw doubt on the viewer's perceptions and thereby throw knowledge into question (1990, 155). This uncertainty generates suspense and stimulates the desire to know more. Moreover, to extend Vera Dika's analysis of the stalker film, the uncertainty generated by the horror film's "gaming attitude" is designed to elicit audience participation (1990, 128), that is, to foster recreational terror.

Henry: Portrait of a Serial Killer extends the pleasure of not-seeing by bringing forcefully into play the pleasure of *not-hearing*. The opening sequence cross-cuts between Henry engaged in the mundane activities of everyday life and a montage of ruined bodies, Henry's victims at the scene of the crime. Each graphic visual track of the aftermath of the crime is overlaid with an acoustic flashback of the violent attack that transpired. The acoustic flashbacks, which only hint at what happened, are muted echoes that function like the play of light and dark in the chiaroscuro tradition. The viewer strains to hear what the muted soundtrack reveals, yet the acoustic flashback withholds clarity. Thus, a partial or blocked acoustic image is juxtaposed with a graphic visual image to play up the dialectic between the pleasure of seeing (more fully) the ruined body, and the pleasure of not (fully) hearing the violence.

The pleasure of not-seeing is not only produced by the activities of the film but also by the activities of the audience. As Giles (1984) notes, audience members often obscure their own line of vision by looking through their hands or by intermittently turning away from the screen. Noting the frequency of this occurrence, Barbara Creed calls the dynamic of not-looking the "fifth look" of cinema and defines it as a distinctive feature of horror spectatorship (1993, 29).[3] In addition, Carol Clover remarks that some viewers cover their ears (1992, 204), no doubt true but far less common that the ones who block their vision. What motivates this act of recoiling from the visual or acoustic image?

Giles accounts for the centrality of these mechanisms of not-seeing by invoking the concept of fetishism, which he distinguishes from Freud's (repr. 1961) definition. According to Freud, fetishism entails a divided attitude whereby the male subject simultaneously retains and abandons the belief that the woman has a penis. He attributes this repudiation of castration to the boy's desire to ward off fears that he too will be castrated by the father. As important as Freud's usage is, it is too narrow for the broad range of fears that the horror film deploys. Giles is right to set aside the question of sexual difference and deal with a more generalized sense of horror. As Giles uses it, fetishism is a blocked vision that recoils from any image of horror. The viewer defends against the "horrible spectacle" and draws pleasure from this defensive activity. The blocked vision"lurks on the threshold" of seeing but "refuses to fully see" (1984, 47).

The refusal to fully see is an act of control exercised by audience members who distance themselves during intense moments of anxiety to keep fear in check when it threatens to overwhelm them. Conversely, the blocked vision produced by the film heightens the intensity of the horror by refusing to show the terrifying spectacle. It does not allow audience members to see even when they look.

The pleasure of recreational terror depends on the tension between not (fully) seeing, the pleasure of recoil, and seeing (more fully), the pleasure of the gaze.[4] What is at stake is seeing, or not-seeing, the monster and the violence that accompanies its appearance. The monster, which is often offscreen or masked, is a conspicuous figure of absence whose very absence incites the desire to see it. As Neale (1980, 44) points out, the monster inevitably appears in the horror film. (A notable exception is *The Haunting*.) The appearance of the monster, whose body is a locus of contradictions, is important to the genre. The monster simultaneously embodies difference through its status as freak or ultimate Other, and erodes difference through its disruption of social categories. Particularly intense moments of the monster's appearance are its initial appearance—its birth, transformation, or entrance—and its destruction, moments invariably marked by violence. Herein lies the importance of the offscreen "star" of the genre, the special-effects artist whose resources are mobilized to effect a terrifying yet realistic appearance (Neale 1980, 45).

The Pleasure of Seeing (More Fully) the Horrifying Spectacle

> If you're bored by it, pretend it's real, but if you're excited by it, pretend it's fake.
>
> —*Bloodsucking Freaks*
> (1976, quoted in Newman 1988, 202)

The realism of special-effects violence, together with audience knowledge that the violence is simulated, operate in tandem to produce a suspension of disbelief. "I know it's not real, but it looks real."[5] The work of special effects, as Boss notes, is to produce a realistic though imperfect "illusion of people in torment" so the artifice can be appreciated and the torment enjoyed (1986, 24). Awareness of artifice, then, is not a flaw but an essential ingredient of recreational terror. The combination of realism and artifice in special-effects violence allows the bored viewer who needs to spike the experience to focus on the realism ("pretend it's real"), while simultaneously allowing the overstimulated viewer verging on terror to focus on the artifice without abandoning a sense of realism ("pretend it's fake"). As recreational terror depends on the tension between seeing and not-seeing, so it depends on the tension between special-effects realism and awareness of its artifice.

This combination of artifice and realism whets viewers' appetites for knowledge about the production process, for a behind-the-scenes look. Fan magazines have emerged to sate this thirst. Prozines, mainstream commercial publications such as *Fangoria* (1979–) or *Cinefantastique* (1970–), and fanzines, amateur publications like *Gore Gazette* are devoted to a discussion of "how they do it."[6] The special-effects discourse stimulates interest in the act of seeing how the effects are produced. Addressed to the competent viewer or fan audience, especially males, these publications yield a discourse that reveals the hidden, behind-the-scenes work, and thus lays bare the artifice involved in production. Fan magazines function to reassure the audience that the monsters of horror film are simulacra, copies without originals, which have "no correspondence in our world" (Telotte 1990, 153) other than the constructions of the special-effects team. They provide a repudiation of the plausibility implicit in special-effects realism. In this vein, Stephen King attributes the commercial failure of *Freaks* (1932) to Tod Browning's use of "real freaks" in the film. "We may only feel really comfortable with horror as long as we can see the zipper running up the monster's back" (1981, 45). The need for this repudiation of plausibility is exacerbated by claims the genre makes that some horror films are based on real-life events. For instance *The Exorcist, The Texas Chain Saw Massacre, The Entity, The Amityville Horror* (1980), and *Henry: Portrait of a Serial Killer* all make such claims.

It is not surprising that the target audience for horror fan magazines is male, since culturally, males are expected to display bravado and unflinching vision, whereas females are expected to cower and look away. The instruction that these magazines provide about special-effects technology allows the fan viewer to distance him or herself from depictions of violence by looking for the trick, e.g., the cut from the actor to the prosthetic device. This strategy of looking for the flaws or ruptures in realism can be seen as a deconstructive operation that allows audience members to enjoy the pleasure of seeing (more fully) without taking the effect so seriously that it becomes too threatening. Looking for ruptures in realism is the counterpart to not-seeing or looking away. Paradoxically, although not-seeing or blocking one's vision to avoid special-effects realism is an act of control exercised by some to reduce anxiety, it also allows the imagination to fill in the gaps and inadvertently enhances the realistic power of the effects. Similarly, fan magazine discourse demystifies the production process for the audience by divulging how special-effects are accomplished, by teaching the audience to see the ruptures in realism, yet it simultaneously effaces the production process by making all the other effects in filmmaking seem natural and thereby heightening the overall realism effect (Stern 1990, 69). Thus, like the framing and lighting techniques of the genre, the special-effects discourse conceals as much as it exposes.

The special-effects magazine, like the horror genre itself, is grounded in the wish to see monsters, mutilated bodies, and mutilation as they "really" are, grounded in the desire "to penetrate 'fictional façades' and glimpse forbidden areas of privacy" (Dervin 1990, 97).[7] This desire to reveal the secrets of the flesh, to expose the hidden, and to penetrate the surface of the body is exemplified in the gore film.

The Wizard of Gore and the Act of Showing

> When people complain of sadism in horror . . . they mean simply that the film is *showing* too much.
>
> —Pirie 1974, 42

The dismembered body, the body in bits and pieces, occupies center stage in the genre. *The Wizard of Gore* (1968), true to its name, is a self-reflexive film that relishes the act of showing the ruined body. Montag the Magnificent, the eponymous wizard, performs mutilation tricks on women who appear fine but who, after leaving the theater, die of injuries like the ones performed on stage. The film opens with a literal show, the stage show of Montag. After staging a few garden variety tricks, Montag launches into a taunting address to the audience on the subject of recreational terror:

> Torture and terror have always fascinated mankind. Perhaps whatever made your predecessors see the sadism of

> the Inquisition and the gore of a gladiator's arena is the same thing that makes you stare at bloody highway accidents and thrill to the terror of death in the bullring. Today, television and films give you the luxury of observing grisly dismemberments and deaths without anyone actually being harmed. But, ladies and gentlemen, have you ever seen the sight of human butchery in person! Well tonight, on this stage, you will have the privilege of seeing such a sight. (my transcription)

This teasing preamble is ostensibly delivered to the fictional audience, but Montag's direct look at the camera overtly addresses the film audience, establishing the first of various links between the two fields of spectatorship. In his speech, Montag sets the stage for the themes that are to be developed in the film. First, he implicates the audience in the impending show of violence, pointing out that they voyeuristically want to see dismemberment and death. Second, he invokes the real (bloody highway accidents) in relation to the illusory (films) and offers to perform the real. Third, he promises to show us "everything," to satiate our desire to see more fully. Nevertheless, after delivering his speech Montag proceeds to guillotine himself on stage to establish the fakeness of the upcoming performance.

The "meat" of the show is standard magician fare with a twist: he (chain) saws a woman from the audience in half. Ironically, although he promises that "nothing will be concealed," he conceals critical points, namely, the hypnotic coercion he exercises on the "volunteer" and the trick he plays on the fictional audience. The volunteer, always female, is first procured by a male audience member and then mesmerized into compliance by Montag. Although the trick he purports to perform is the *illusion* of sawing a woman in half when she is in fact unharmed, the *real* trick is that he is sawing a woman in half and she only appears to be unharmed. In effect, he performs the illusion of an illusion, while the guillotine, signifier of fakeness, looms in the background. Further, while it appears to the fictional audience that he is dispassionately waving his hands over her body, he is in fact lasciviously fondling her entrails, a sight available only to the privileged film audience. The trick seemingly ends when she walks off stage, but it "really" only ends when her (already dead) body collapses in a bloody heap after leaving the performance.

This is the first in a series of repetitive performances in which the female body becomes the broken body, sundered by a battery of phallic instruments: chain saw, metal spike, punch press, and sword. Each time, the film audience is privileged to see what is "really" happening. The scene crosscuts between the harmless trick discernible to the fictional audience, the destruction of the woman's body visible to the film audience, and the fictional audience impassively watching the performance. The fictional audience's reaction is disconcertingly juxtaposed to shots of blood and viscera. The editing presents the action twice, in jump cuts that alternate between the varying perspectives of the two audiences. Musical codes mark the transition from one perspective to the other and thus facilitate the process of looking at the innocuous shots while looking away from the violent ones, for those viewers who elect to not-see. Although this strategy might appear to augment audience safety, what it does is decidedly disturbing; it aligns the film audience member who does not look with a fictional audience that complacently watches but does not see the torture and murder of the women.

Just as *The Wizard of Gore* brings to the fore the position of the audience, so it highlights the artifice of its special effects, and indeed all its effects, through the production of unnaturalness. Although the film bears the stamp of documentary realism (out-of-focus shots, inaudible dialogue, out-of-sync postdubbing, Montag's speech to the audience via a direct look at the camera), it more forcefully strains realism through wooden acting, continuity violations, seedy sets, unmotivated action, and narrative inconsistencies. In particular, the dialogue makes excessive claims about the damage done to the women's bodies. Women are said to be mashed to a pulp, punch-pressed from head to foot, decapitated, cut in half. But the dialogue claims exceed the trauma we see inflicted on the bodies, either through the privileged vision of the film audience during the performance, or in the aftermath when the broken body is revealed to all. For instance, when the body of the "decapitated" woman is snatched from the morgue by Montag, he slings her over his shoulder—head intact. Thus, the dialogue's excessive claims substitute for adequacy of vision, the very thing the film purports to deliver by showing us "everything." Ironically, this film which privileges the act of showing relies heavily on the act of telling.

Based on audience reactions to a video screening for students at the State University of New York at Purchase in 1990, I would argue that despite the exceedingly poor quality of the special effects, the powerfully disturbing ideas behind the effects allow the film to pack a wallop of the "You've got to be fucking kidding!" variety of which Brophy speaks (1986, 11).[8] The response expresses incredulity and disgust in equal measure at the excess of the body horror aroused by the special effects. For instance, when Montag hammers a railroad spike into the skull of the second victim, it is comically clear that he is violating a mannequin. But the audience still squirms in dread and disgust when he bores his finger into the hole to draw out brain tissue and gouges out her eyes.

The primacy of the ruined-body-as-spectacle is central to *The Wizard of Gore*. Boss, following Brophy, claims that the appeal of body horror lies in the fact that it allows the audience to rehearse the loss of control over the body through gory special effects. Everything else is subordinated to the exigency of showing the spectacle of human carnage (1986, 15). *The Wizard of Gore* quite literally locates the ravaged spectacle at center stage. Each performance lingers over the organs and blood that spill from the despoiled body. The film displays the horror genre's obsession with the body in bits and pieces. The image of the mutilated body transformed into an unrecognizable morass suggests the degree to which the body has become the focus of acute anxiety in the postmodern horror film.

Carnography

This obsession with the body suggests a connection between horror and pornography, one critics have noted before

(Williams 1989b, Clover 1992). The horror film, like pornography, dares not only to violate taboos but to expose the secrets of the flesh, to spill the contents of the body. If pornography is the genre of the wet dream, then horror is the genre of the wet death.[9] They each whet the appetites of their respective and overlapping audiences for more, as video rental receipts and the proliferation of remakes and sequels attest. The link between hard-core pornography and hard-core horror or the gore film is captured in the term "carnography" (Gehr 1990, 58), which uses the carnality of both genres as a bridge.[10]

It is this very carnality that relegates hard core and gore to the status of disreputable genres. As Richard Dyer points out about porn, both are disreputable genres because they engage the viewer's body (1985, 27), elicit physical responses such as fear, disgust, and arousal in indeterminate combinations, and thereby privilege the degraded half of the mind-body split. When academic critics engage these genres in an intellectual fashion, they typically issue disclaimers about "prurient fascination" (Tudor 1989, 60) in order to avoid "contamination" by a "filthy subject" (Williams 1989a, xi).[11]

These disreputable genres violate taboos by privileging the act of showing the body, by figuring what Clover calls "the 'opened' body" (1992, 32). They expose what is normally concealed or encased to reveal the hidden recesses of the body, porn through carnal knowledge and horror through carnage. Porn and horror are obsessed with the transgression of bodily boundaries. Both are concerned with the devouring orifice. But whereas pornography is concerned with the phallic penetration and secretions of sexually coded orifices like the mouth (gaping in ecstasy or pain), vagina, and anus, horror is more concerned with the creation of openings where there were none before.

The narratives of both genres, sometimes thin sometimes dense, surround spectacles of the penetration or devouring of a body. Each film is a series of repetitions and variations on this central theme. The excessive narrative and specular redundancy of both genres is further constructed on an intertextual level through the proliferation of remakes and sequels that dominate the marketplace. In pornography, this central theme is played out principally through the "meat shot," penetration by a penis in close-up (Williams 1989a, 72), an appellation that seems exceedingly appropriate to the horror film's obsession with visual evidence of "the 'opened' body," from the pierced to the eviscerated body, from the gashed to the sundered limb. The term "meat shot" is also suggestive of the body's role in films about cannibalism, from the raw meat of *Night of the Living Dead* to the cooked and commercially profitable chili of *Texas Chain Saw Massacre II* (1986).

The penetration and devouring of the body that the meat shot thematizes results in the loss of body fluids, culminating in the involuntary spasm of orgasm, *le petit mort* ("the little death"), performed in porn or the literal death performed in horror. In pornography, the involuntary spasm is captured in the "money shot," or cum shot, in which the penetrating man pulls out so as to ejaculate in plain sight, the highly staged visual proof of spontaneous male pleasure (Williams 1989a, 101). The visual proof of female pleasure is indirect, communicated through her moans, cries, and the contortions of her face and body.[12] In horror, the involuntary spasm is the death of the penetrated or devoured body accompanied by screaming and bleeding, the visual proof of violation. Unlike porn, in horror it is the penetrated body of the victim that shudders and bleeds producing the visual evidence of violation.

Both genres show the body in bits and pieces. Pornography does so largely through the use of extreme close-ups like the meat shot and the money shot, whereas gore utilizes both close-ups (of wounds, weapons) and the literal spectacle of the body in bits and pieces (dismembered limbs, exposed viscera).

Although both genres claim to expose "everything," there are limits to what they will show. The decisive difference between pornography and horror lies in their disparate claims to facticity. As Linda Williams points out, the pleasure of pornography is assumed to be real, i.e., involuntary and unfeigned. The genre is obsessed with the cum shot precisely because it is the visible *proof* of male pleasure. In contrast, the pain of horror is assumed to be fake (1989b, 42). Horror relies on the realistic, but insistently simulated, representation of violence. The *proof* of this lies in the discourse of spe-

FIGURE 2.1. The body in bits and pieces occupies center stage in the contemporary horror film, as the charnel house imagery of *The Texas Chain Saw Massacre* (1974) shows. Courtesy of Museum of Modern Art Film Stills Archive.

cial effects that flaunts the technological ability to offer the violent spectacle.

When the reality principle of pornography is conjoined with the mutilation principle of horror, a different order of film is constituted, not horror but the snuff film. As an analytic category, snuff refers to films in which women are actually killed during sex. Belief in the existence of the snuff film gained credibility with the release of *Snuff* (1976), which uses the violent special effects of horror but makes false claims about the facticity of its violence. It is because the sex scenes in *Snuff* mark it as pornography that the violence and pain could also be read as real (Williams 1989a, 190–92).[13] Snuff, unlike horror, exceeds the limits of realism; in snuff, the violence and pain are real.[14]

Another asymmetry, this one at the level of the audience, marks a crucial distinction between porn and horror. The viewer of pornography is encouraged, indeed expected, to bring his wet dream to fruition, to produce his own ejaculatory emission with or without penetration, whereas the viewer of horror is neither encouraged nor expected to participate in murder, mutilation, or blood letting. The wet death is intended to remain in the realm of fantasy. This is why the snuff film, marked as both a pornographic vehicle to orgasm, and a "real" document of murder poses such a profound threat. It is arguably a filmic incitement to commit murder. Although horror is not snuff, I suggest that the similarities between horror and porn, particularly their aim to affect the body of the viewer contributes to some critics' willingness to charge that violent horror films trigger violent behavior. The slippage between genres underlies the slippage from affect to effect in this allegation.

An essential ingredient of the horror genre is the simulated character of its violence. As far as the horror genre is concerned, the terrain of the snuff film is *terra incognita*. Snuff surpasses the limits of horror. Yet in deference to the genre's drive to violate boundaries, some horror films display a fascination with snuff. Just as some horror films stage the (improbable if not impossible) murder of audience members during a horror film screening, so some horror films stage the murder of cast members during production. *Videodrome* (1983) features a cable channel in which people are tortured to death in real time, the ultimate hard-core S&M channel. *Peeping Tom* (1960) draws together pornography and snuff in the character of Mark who moonlights as a pornographic photographer but whose real passion is murder. Mark kills women who live off the sexual display of their bodies (prostitute, actress/dancer, model) by stabbing them with the spike on the end of his tripod, as he captures their final terrified moments on film. Each murder is recorded and becomes part of his documentary, his faces of death. Mark avidly replays his snuff film. Similarly, in *Henry, Portrait of a Serial Killer*, Henry videotapes the murder of a family, and his partner in crime watches it obsessively. This cross-genre fascination is a self-reflexive move that pushes the boundaries of the genre by playing with the cardinal rule of recreational terror that violence be simulated. It is the simulated character of violence in the horror film that makes it possible to play with the spectacle of body horror.

Body Horror

Why is the genre obsessed with body horror, with the spectacle of the body in bits and pieces? The postmodern horror film draws a universe out of control where extreme violence is endemic and virtually unstoppable. The presentation of violence as a constituent of everyday life produces an unstable and paranoid universe in which familiar categories collapse. The body figures as the site of this collapse. Violence is random, yet specifically aimed against the body to produce an "intimate apocalypse" (Boss 1986, 17). The genre rehearses the fear of injury (not only castration but all mutilation) and death in a world where safety in every sense of the term is a fiction.

The audience encounters the genre with the expectation of experiencing recreational terror. To do so, the audience draws upon its reserves of insider knowledge gleaned from a history of viewing the genre and sometimes by reading special-effects magazines and film reviews to both mitigate and hone the terror of the experience. It is as much an exercise in mastery as it is an exercise in terror. Even the genre's refusal of narrative closure becomes through repetition domesticated and eventually anticipated. (After a theater screening of *Species* [1995] that I attended, conversation in the women's bathroom revolved around disappointment that the ending revealed a monstrous rat rather than a hitherto undetected surviving offspring.) It is comforting for viewers to know that they underwent an ordeal and had the mettle to survive it. Moreover, because they are not overcome by the extremity of the fiction, viewers are reassured that as bad as things are in reality, they could be infinitely worse.

Recreational terror is the context in which viewers submit to the tension and fear provoked by body horror, a highly conventionalized spectacle of violence in which controlled loss substitutes for the loss of control that people who come to these films are already experiencing. Or as Wes Craven put it when asked about why people go to horror films: "I don't think people like to be scared. I think people *are* scared or have been scared."[15] In the horror film viewing experience, fear becomes both master and subject. As Brophy so aptly describes it: "The pleasure of the text is . . . getting the shit scared out of you—and loving it; an exchange mediated by adrenalin" (1986, 5). Both mastery and submission are at work in the construction of pleasure.

Creed provides a different interpretation of what it means when someone says that a horror film "scared the shit out of me." For Creed, viewing a horror film entails a double movement. First there is the desire to see "sickening, horrific images" that disrupt social categories, a process she describes as "pleasure in perversity" (1993, 10). Then there is the inverse desire to "throw up" or repel these monstrous images when they threaten the spectator's sense of bodily integrity. By momentarily looking away from these anxiety-inducing images, the spectator is able to redraw the boundary that separates her or him from the fictional body in bits and pieces, thereby mitigating the encounter with the monstrous and reasserting control (1993, 28–29). But the withdrawal of which she speaks is only partial since the not-seeing "spectator" is still vulnerable to a soundtrack engineered to enhance fear.

Creed's account emphasizes the spectator's need to defend against extreme terror, but she disregards the degree to which not-seeing works to heighten anxiety. When a viewer looks away not only does s/he not see the artifice of special-effects work, but her or his imagination fills in the gap to produce a potentially more terrifying image. Although Creed acknowledges the pleasure implicit in looking at taboo or monstrous images, she subordinates this pleasure to the overriding desire to expel the monstrous Other that threatens to disrupt the symbolic order (1993, 37). As Creed sees it, the horror film functions to restore the symbolic order and repress the taboo.

To make this argument, Creed disregards two crucial elements of the postmodern horror film. First is the de rigueur open ending built into both the film text and the sequel structure of the marketplace. Second is the pleasure viewers, especially female viewers, gain from seeing however partially or temporarily the overturning or disintegration of the symbolic order. Unlike Creed, who all too easily subordinates "pleasure in perversity" to the desire to expel the monstrous, William Paul's discussion of "gross-out" sustains the tension between attraction and repulsion implicit in body horror. As he puts it, "gross-out always implies an ambivalence because it is founded on attraction to that which repulses, or more precisely it inverts normal values to acknowledge an attraction in revulsion" (1994, 312). Disgust carries with it desire. Creed's double movement slides too readily from pleasure in perversion to the closed ending of throwing up the monstrous.

In a much less sophisticated manner, Twitchell makes a similar argument. Twitchell views the horror film as a morality tale, a socializing ritual for adolescents that induces the repression of violence and directs sexuality into conservative, heteromonogamous channels (1985, 66). Although writing in the eighties, Twitchell's antiquated sense of the horror film is that it is largely unchanged. He reduces films such as *Halloween* to new renditions of old myths (1985, 54). For Twitchell, the traditional figures of Dracula, Frankenstein, and Hyde are the still relevant archetypal forms who embody the sexual confusion and anxieties of adolescence (1985,

104).[16] For instance, Hyde represents the eruption of untrammeled sexuality, a change marked by the growth of body hair in unaccustomed places. Twitchell analyzes these narratives to illustrate how they punish transgressive, nonreproductive sexuality, including promiscuous, incestuous, homosexual, or masturbatory sexuality. By staging figurative versions of these transgressive sexualities and defining them as having the power to "melt down the nuclear family," horror socializes adolescents to avert these temptations (1985, 104). Thus deviance reinforces the androcentric status quo and serves a normative, stabilizing function.

The problem with both Twitchell and Creed's interpretations is that they purge the horror viewing experience of the glee with which viewers relish the nastiness of "sickening, horrific images." To explore the appeal of "melt[ing] down the nuclear family" would violate Twitchell's investment in the male-dominated social order which he expressly endorses. And though Creed treats feminine monstrosity, or as she calls it, the monstrous-feminine, as the historical product of a male-dominated social order of which she is critical, she fails to consider the transgressive pleasures of the violent female for female viewers.

CHAPTER THREE

. . . And Then She Killed Him: Women and Violence in the Slasher Film

Pleasure and Danger

Dancing through the minefield of the contemporary horror film, with its bloody display of the all-too-often female body in bits and pieces, is fraught with danger for women. But pleasure shares the field with danger. Unfortunately, for the female viewer accused of masochism or the female fan labeled an apologist for a woman-hating genre, there is no room for pleasure; only danger is accommodated. But there is more to be gained by approaching the question of female spectatorship of horror by keeping both pleasure and danger in play. It is a move especially suited to this transgressive genre and to the contested question of female spectatorship at hand. Female spectatorship of horror is a much neglected and misunderstood topic, but like other taboo pleasures before it, the pleasure women derive from watching horror films deserves to be explored.

The horror film's construction of recreational terror produces a pleasurable encounter with violence and danger. But the assumption of much critical writing is that these pleasures

---

The idea for this title comes from a suggestion Kimberly Flynn made circa 1987 (personal communication) for a feminist film series featuring films in which women kill men and get away with it, to be called ". . . And Then She Killed Him."

are the preserve of men. Women are either absent or cringing in distress. In "The Terror of Pleasure" Tania Modleski (163) contends that "[popular horror films] enable the male spectator to distance himself somewhat from the terror. And, as usual, it is the female spectator who is *truly* deprived of 'solace and pleasure.'" Similarly, in "When the Woman Looks" Linda Williams limits pleasure in viewing horror films to men: "Whenever the movie screen holds a particularly effective image of terror, little boys and grown men make it a point of honor to look, while little girls and grown women cover their eyes or hide behind the shoulders of their dates" (83). Williams fails to recognize the pleasure of not-seeing, and both she and Modleski assume that the female viewer derives no comparable pleasure from the contemporary horror film since female mutilation and murder figure so prominently in the genre.

In *Men, Women and Chain Saws: Gender in the Modern Horror Film*, Carol Clover advances the idea that the primary pleasure for male viewers of the genre is a masochistic rather than a sadistic one, but her concern with gender is strictly limited to male viewers. In *The Monstrous-Feminine: Film, Feminism, Psychoanalysis*, Barbara Creed, who turns her attention to female monstrosity, maintains that the monstrous-feminine in the horror film speaks to men about their fear of women, but she has little to say about how it might speak to women about female power. Both books center the male viewer and neglect the question of female audience pleasure in the horror film. This question has by now become a structuring absence of horror film criticism.

My discussion of the horror film is motivated by a desire to disrupt the facile assumption that the genre does not speak *to* women but only *about* them, and that it does this in a degrading manner. The postmodern horror film's routine staging of the spectacle of the ruined body, particularly the female body, calls for a feminist analysis. Moreover, the historical conjunction between the emergence of the postmodern horror film and the advent of the second wave American feminist movement in the early seventies begs the question: How have feminist protest and antifeminist backlash informed the character of the contemporary horror film?

The feminist movement, founded on the imperative that women must be free to control their own bodies, has repeatedly drawn attention to the issue of violence against women, including representational violence. Although rarely heralded as feminist, horror films, for instance *Dressed to Kill*, have been the object of feminist opprobrium, not unlike pornography, charged with promoting violence against women by staging the spectacle of the ruined *female* body. This attack, leveled with particular fervor against the slasher subgenre inaugurated by *Halloween* (1978), found widespread expression in the popular press (Ebert 1981; Maslin 1982). The criticism popularized by this discourse is that women are graphically and gratuitously victimized in the horror film, a genre excoriated for misogyny. This discourse is peopled with sadistic male viewers who enjoy reviling images and principled feminists who abhor the same. It leaves no room for the pleasure of female viewers, particularly feminists, except as masochists or sex traitors.

Although I agree that it matters what representations of women abound in culture, the tendency to see the horror film as monolithically destructive of female subjectivity overlooks the contradictory dynamics within the genre as well as the complexity with which audiences respond to it. The antihorror discourse sees only how the genre has been formed by antifeminist backlash but overlooks how feminism has informed the genre. The horror film is a contradictory form that must be understood in all its complexity lest we misinterpret popular culture or underestimate its subversive potential.

The Slasher Film

A hotbed of contention in feminist debates, the slasher film is the most disreputable form of the horror film. Excoriated for gratuitous and misogynous violence, this subgenre has caught the disparaging eye of commercial critics like Roger Ebert, the scrutiny of social scientists like Daniel Linz, and the ambivalent attention of academic critics like Vera Dika,[1]

Clover, and Creed, who have written books about the contemporary horror film.[2]

The disreputability of the genre, to which critics invariably allude, is related to its importance. Robin Wood (1978) argues that the disreputability of the horror genre carries with it the agreement that these films are not to be taken seriously, a stance conducive to the free play of repressed emotions. Similarly, Clover privileges the genre because it is disreputable. She argues that the horror genre is important because it engages repressed fears and desires through the reenactment of conflict (11).

Clover (26) periodizes the slasher film from 1974 to 1986, thus drawing on a broader temporal framework than Dika who limits her discussion to the height of the slasher film's popularity—1978 to 1981. Both argue that the slasher film is characterized by a formulaic combination of cinematic, narrative, and stylistic elements. Cinematically, the films are low-budget productions with a largely adolescent audience. Dika (9) puts the age group at 12 to 17; Clover (1987, 224) puts it at 12 to 20. Clover, like most critics, asserts that "by all accounts" the audience for the slasher film is predominantly male (1987, 192), whereas Dika contends that it is largely (55 percent) female (87). Although Dika's assertion about the composition of the audience is an interesting departure, she arrives at this figure through a statistical misreading (1990, 142). Moreover, she does not consider the implications of female spectatorship.[3]

Drawing on Dika and Clover's discussions, the slasher narrative can be summarized as follows: A masked or hidden (largely offscreen) psychotic male propelled by psychosexual fury stalks and kills a sizeable number of young women and men with a high level of violence. The killer's rage derives from a traumatic childhood experience, which is recounted chronologically (e.g., *Halloween*) or in flashback (e.g., *Friday the 13th*). The killer returns to the scene of the past event to reenact the violence. Although both women and men are killed, the stalking and killing of women is stressed. After a protracted struggle, a resourceful female usually subdues the killer, sometimes kills him, and survives.

Stylistically, distinctive elements are employed to narrativize the stalking and slashing. Since the killer is offscreen or masked for most of the film, his presence is signified by musical codes and a battery of distinctive shots, namely, the unclaimed POV shot and the solitary reaction shot that figure so prominently in producing the pleasure of not-seeing. One of the most-cited examples of this camera work is the opening of *Halloween*, a five-minute sequence done in two long takes which bears further description.

A tracking shot approaches a suburban house. The stalker climbs the front steps and moves around the house to peer voyeuristically through a window at a teenage couple engaged in foreplay. When the couple goes upstairs, the stalker enters the house through the back door into the kitchen. An out-of-focus arm enters the frame to open a drawer and remove a butcher knife. This is the first clear evidence we have that the perspective belongs to a narrative character. The stalker lurks in the shadows when the teenage boy comes downstairs (mere moments after going up) and exits the house, then goes upstairs where he retrieves a clown mask from the floor and puts it on. Our vision is now circumscribed by the outline of the mask. He approaches the half-nude teenage girl as she brushes her hair before the mirror. He observes the rumpled sheets on the bed and begins to stab her. From his perspective we see the motion of his arm swinging as he stabs her until she collapses to the floor. Then he retraces his footsteps down the stairs, goes out the front door and down the steps. A car pulls up and an adult couple gets out. When the man removes the mask we see the killer for the first time: a dazed six-year-old boy holding a bloody knife. The end of the sequence is marked by the abdication of the unclaimed POV shot in favor of a reverse shot showing us the killer. Just as this sequence establishes within the film that the reappearance of the unclaimed point of view shot and its musical code signifies the killer's presence, so *Halloween* establishes this set of visual and musical codes as conventions for the slasher film.

This voyeuristic camera work locates the viewer in a masterful position; it sets up a disjunction between the privileged knowledge of spectators and the limited knowledge of narrative characters. But the genre's preoccupation with not-seeing limits the audience's vision even at the moment when the viewer's vision is aligned with the stalker's, since the foreground objects that construct the voyeuristic keyhole simultaneously obscure the viewer/voyeur's line of sight. Further, this camera work masks not only the killer's identity but also his whereabouts. Its movement is unfettered by the limits of a human body. Although these shots are coded as subjective, it is sometimes ambiguous whether or not they represent the point of view of any narrative character, producing what Giles calls "empty visions" (1984, 42). This variant of the camera work functions to gull us, as when it is shown to represent the point of view of a nonthreatening narrative character or, as in the opening sequence of *Halloween*, when it misrepresents the killer's perspective by conveying the gaze from adult height. By withholding information and providing misleading clues, the system of looks validates paranoia as a legitimate epistemological position. Evil lurks in what we cannot see, and we cannot trust what we do see.

A weighty argument for the misogyny of the slasher film is that the voyeuristic camera work which keeps the killer offscreen during much of the stalking and slashing also aligns the viewer with the killer's point of view. If, as many critics who cite anecdotal evidence assert (Clover 1987, 224; 1992, 6–7; Caputi 1990, 9), the horror film audience is primarily male,[4] then this camera work locates largely male viewers in a sadistic position, especially vis-à-vis female victims. Like the woman in Laura Mulvey's seminal essay, "Visual Pleasure and Narrative Cinema," victims in the slasher film are positioned through the male gaze as objects of sexual investigation: surveyed and eroticized before they are killed.[5] The visual evidence of their sexual activity is used to establish their guilt and to motivate the punishment for their transgressions. What Clover (33) calls "the postcoital death" is a staple of many slasher films.

Like the woman in Mulvey's essay, victims are symbolically castrated. Unable to look, speak, or hear authoritatively, victims lack knowledge of the threat. Unable to use violence, and thus drive the narrative forward, victims lack narrative agency. We do not see the killer from their point of view but rather from the killer's point of view, we see them as scrutinized sexual objects who become "objects of aggression." Their symbolic castration is acted out, made literal in the mutilation that turns a victim into a wound (Dika 101, 90). And the spectacle of the "bleeding wound," to use Mulvey's (1985, 305) term, is disproportionately female.

Indeed, a compelling argument for the misogyny of the horror genre is the different character of male and female death. Although victims of both genders are objects of sexual investigation, and despite the evenhandedness of many slasher films in which roughly equal numbers of men and women are killed, male and female death are not the same. As Clover (35) argues, male death is swifter, more distanced, and more likely to occur offscreen or to be obscured, whereas female death is extended, occurs at close range, and in graphic detail. Her death, and the anticipation of her death, occupies substantially more screen time and is more erotically charged than that of her male counterpart.

We see this dynamic played out in *Halloween*. Of the two male victims, one is killed offscreen (his death is incidental), and the other is dispatched quickly in the shadowy kitchen. Although he is the object of aggression, he is not shown to be the object of the gaze before the attack. Although his is a postcoital death, it occupies substantially less screen time and drama than his girlfriend's death. The three female victims have either just engaged in sexual intercourse or are about to do so. It is disconcerting to note that women are killed because they are female to a degree that it cannot be said that men are killed because they are male (Clover 34). Indeed, like film noir, the slasher film regards female sexuality with a marked degree of fear and loathing.

But to reduce the mechanics of the genre to this gender-polarized formulation is to ignore the female character, whom Clover aptly names the "Final Girl," who survives the onslaught to which most of the other characters, male and female, succumb. The surviving female is distinguished from the victims by being allotted more close-ups, screen time, and reverse shots from her perspective. Her character is more fully developed, and she is less likely to be the object of sexual scrutiny, less subject to the controlling gaze (Dika 89, 91). Like the killer, she is able to see, hear, and speak authoritatively. Like the viewer, she directs an active investigative gaze at the events surrounding her and so comes to understand the magnitude of the violence that threatens her (Clover 48, 35). Like the viewer, the surviving female adopts paranoia as a valid position from which to know. She trusts her misgivings and keeps her eyes open; she exercises what Judith Halberstam calls "productive fear" (1995, 126–27). Because the surviving female is conscious of being watched, she becomes watchful. Her ability to look is crucial because it enables her to subject the killer to her controlling gaze, and thus to transform him into an object of aggression and herself into an agent of violence.

By Any Means Necessary

The surviving female's appropriation of the gaze enables her to use violence to defend herself effectively and to drive the narrative forward.[6] We see *him* from *her* point of view. Indeed, the transition from the killer's point of view to the surviving female's point of view, which increases progressively in the second part of the film, is a pivotal shift that motivates audience identification with the surviving female (Clover 45). This shift in perspective culminates in the protracted struggle between the surviving female and the killer, which constitutes the climax of the film. During this sequence she is "abject terror personified" (Clover 35). Preyed upon, tormented, and terrorized, she is pushed to the limit and driven to fight *by any means necessary*. The surviving female faces the daunting task of fighting a virtually indestructible attacker hell-bent on killing her, one who will not stay dead. She stabs him with a knife, hacks him with an ax, bludgeons him with a tree limb, lances him with a pitchfork, and gashes him with a chain saw. She fights with courage, resourcefulness, intelligence, and competence. In *Halloween*, Laurie bends a wire coathanger to jab the killer in the eye, thus piercing the opening in his protective mask. In *A Nightmare on Elm Street*, Nancy rigs up a series of booby traps using household devices and lures the killer into her trap. In *The Stepfather*, Stephanie fashions a knife from a broken shard of glass.

Not only does she fashion weapons, the surviving female runs, screams, cries out for help, dodges blows, negotiates,[7] and fights back with anything at her disposal. In other words, she employs the range of strategies which sociologists Pauline Bart and Patricia O'Brien (1984) argue are most effective in avoiding rape. When one strategy or weapon fails, she tries another, improvising from the materials and openings at hand. The most misogynous of the slasher films (e.g., *The Entity*) invariably play down this feminist element of the genre. But despite its misogynous inclinations, it must be acknowledged that horror, especially the slasher film, consistently shows women using self-defense effectively.[8]

This pattern has prevailed over time. Clover (37) observes a shift from earlier films like *The Texas Chain Saw Massacre* (1974) and *Halloween* (1978), where in the end women are saved by the intervention of men, to later films like *Friday the 13th* (1980), *The Slumber Party Massacre* (1982), *The Texas Chain Saw Massacre Part 2* (1986), and *The Stepfather* (1987), where women must rely on themselves to kill the killer and survive. The ascendance of this feature is borne out in the 1990 remake of *Night of the Living Dead*, where Barbra, virtually catatonic in the 1968 version, emerges in the remake as a fully self-reliant survivor.[9] Moreover, this narrative convention has been appropriated by mainstream cinema. For instance, the resourceful female protagonists of *Copycat* (1995), *The Silence of the Lambs* (1991), *Sleeping with the Enemy* (1991), and *Blue Steel* (1990) rescue themselves from murderous male psychotics by killing their pursuers at the conclusion of a protracted stalking sequence. Before Thelma and Louise there were Nancy and Stephanie and about a hundred other young women who fought back in the excoriated slasher film.

To see the slasher film as an unmitigated celebration of male-on-female violence for a male audience is to ignore not

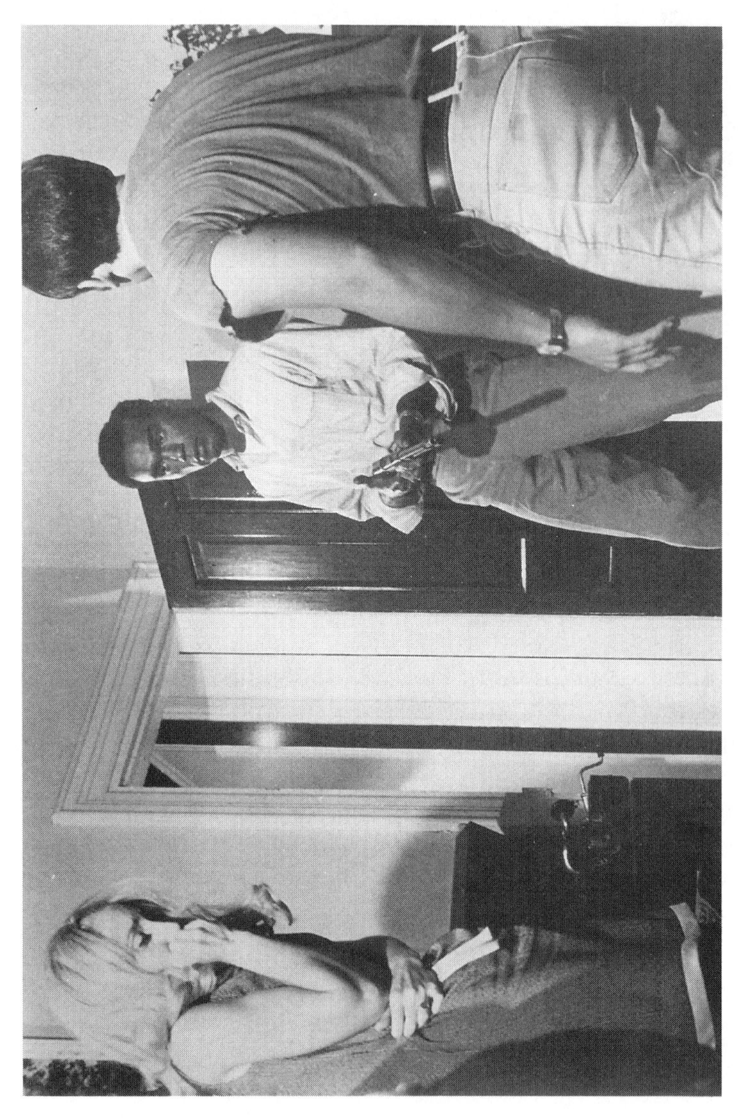

FIGURE 3.1. In *Night of the Living Dead* (1968), Barbra is virtually catatonic. Courtesy of Museum of Modern Art Film Stills Archive.

FIGURE 3.2. Whereas in the 1990 remake of *Night of the Living Dead* the character of Barbara emerges as a self-reliant survivor who fights back by any means necessary. Courtesy of Museum of Modern Art Film Stills Archive.

only the surviving female but the female psychotic. Since the horror genre hinges on violating audience expectations, one variant of the twist ending is to cast a woman as monster, as in *Friday the 13th*. The female psychotic is an example of what Creed (1993, 1) calls the "monstrous-feminine." Unlike Clover and Dika who focus on woman as the victim of the monster, Creed's focus is on woman as monster. Like Mulvey, she subscribes to the Freudian notion that women arouse castration anxiety in men, but questions that this is so simply because men perceive women as castrated. Creed contends that women strike terror in the hearts of men because men perceive women as castrating, a fear played out in intercourse as "the penis 'disappears' inside the woman's 'devouring mouth'" (Creed 6 quoting Lurie 1982, 55). In marked contrast to Clover, Creed argues that far from allaying male fears, the slasher film works to keep castration anxiety alive in male viewers through the dual characterization of woman as castrated victim and castrating heroine (127). Indeed, a substantial portion of the violence that the slasher film celebrates is female-on-male retaliatory violence.

Further, to see the slasher film as an unmitigated celebration of male-on-female violence for a male audience overlooks the capacity of male viewers to identify with the female survivor. Through subjective camera work, the slasher film structures some measure of identification with both the voyeuristic killer whose violence drives the narrative, and with the surviving female in her vulnerability as she acts out the viewer's fear of injury, death, and the unknown, as well as in her violence as she turns her own fury against the attacker. Through fantasy, the viewer can identify with a variety of viewpoints, including different-gender characters and positions that exceed the identity the viewer holds consciously (Cowie 1984). This multiplicity and shifting of identifications is not a "problem" for the audience; on the contrary, it is at the heart of the experience and the pleasure of the genre.

Clover, who insists on the male character of the horror audience, presents a convincing argument that the male viewer identifies as much with the surviving female's abject terror as with her heroism, her ability to use violence in self-defense and to drive the narrative forward. Far from being an exclusively sadistic experience where male viewers derive pleasure from identification with the brutal killer, especially with the violence he directs against women, the slasher-film viewing experience is one that shifts between sadistic and masochistic registers to tell "both sides of the story" (12). What is the story that is being told? Clover's commitment to a psychoanalytic and figurative reading of the story, together with her singular focus on the male audience, produces an oedipal story: The slasher film dramatizes the male viewer's incestuous sadomasochistic fantasy of having sex with his father, but the desired and dreaded erotic penetration is displaced onto violence and onto a female body (51–52). This drama is played out by the surviving female who stands in for the male adolescent viewer. Her femaleness serves to distance him from the taboo nature of the fantasy being enacted in the film. It is this need to shield the male viewer from the homosexual nature of his desires that motivates the suviving female's sexual inactivity (1987, 212). In Clover's scenario, the powerful female is underneath it all a male in drag.

Gender Trouble

Judith Butler tells us that when there is a culturally defined ill fit between anatomical sex, gender identity, and gender performance, as we have in drag, there is gender trouble (1990, 337–38). The surviving female's narrative agency produces a dissonance between these three dimensions of embodiedness. This gender trouble motivates Dika and Clover's characterization of the surviving female as masculine or boyish. The surviving female shares with the killer what Dika describes as the *masculine* ability to look and to wield violence (91). Clover designates "[h]er smartness, gravity, competence in mechanical and other practical matters" as evidence of her "boyish" character, further spelled out in names like Stevie, Marti, and Stretch (40).

What does the "masculinization" of the surviving female signify? Broadly speaking, it signifies the horror genre's inscription within a male-dominant discourse where power is coded as masculine, even when embodied in biological females.[10] Active desire and aggression are the prerogatives of masculinity. Within the terms of this discourse feminine means passive, so feminine agency is an oxymoron. Clover and Dika tacitly accept these terms in their characterization of the surviving female as masculine and their reduction of agency to masculinity. Smartness, gravity, competence, and the ability to fight are only prerogatives of the masculine in a male-dominated society.

Moreover, in the "masculinization" of the surviving female lurks the specter of the lesbian. Lynda Hart argues in *Fatal Women: Lesbian Sexuality and the Mark of Aggression* (xi) that representations of violent women are steeped in anxiety about lesbians. Because violence is gendered male, the violent woman is defined as masculine. Hart notes that historically the lesbian has been defined more by her aggressiveness than by her sexual object choice (1994, 9). As a woman who usurps the masculine prerogatives of aggression and the gaze, the surviving female shares an affinity with the lesbian.

In a male-dominated social order only men do the violent things the surviving female does; therefore, within the terms of hegemonic discourse she is not really female. This is what compels Clover to read the Final Girl as a male in drag. Writing about the popular press's reception of *Thelma and Louise* (1991), a mainstream film about women who kill, Hart summarized it thus: "This representation is not really about women; it is about men. Now you see women, now you don't" (74). But her words could just as easily apply to Clover's analysis of the surviving female. Hart continues: "What is it that we *are* seeing when we see women who are *not really* women but are perhaps 'really men'? One answer," Clover's answer, "would be the projection of male fantasies,"[11] but another answer is that women who are "really men" are lesbians (74).

What is at stake when the femaleness of the survivor is reduced to her display of abject terror, and agency is relegated to masculinity? Nothing less than the impossibility of female agency within this formulation. Clover's reading builds on the work of Mulvey and others who ground their analysis of film on a psychoanalytic model of sexual difference that defines heterosexuality as the norm. Within this model what varies is the active (masculine) or passive (feminine) character of heterosexual desire. Within the binary logic of this framework, active female desire can only be defined as a masculinized position.[12] The upshot of this model is the erasure of the lesbian ("women who are *not really* women but are perhaps 'really men'") or any active female subject.

Patricia White questions feminist film theory's slavish devotion to the heterosexual binary and suggests at what price this allegiance is maintained. She notes with dismay that when theory is caught within the "binary stranglehold of sexual difference" (White 1992, 136) the female subject of film is reduced to what Mulvey (1981, 12) calls the "masculinization of the spectator position." By describing the surviving female as masculine Clover capitulates to the "binary stranglehold of sexual difference." But more to the point, by characterizing her as a boy in drag, Clover resituates female viewers who identify with the (for once) female agent of violence as male-identified.

Although Clover acknowledges that women may read the films in a more female-empowering manner than her reading allows (54), she too uncritically accepts the literary model that "those who save themselves are male, and those who are saved by others are female" (59). If a woman cannot be aggressive and still be a woman, then female agency is a pipe dream. But if the surviving female can be aggressive and be *really* a woman, then she subverts this binary notion of gender that buttresses male dominance. Clover dismisses the progressive potential of this gender trouble. Instead, she derisively characterizes the genre's transgression of gender boundaries as an outgrowth of the "massive gender confusion" generated by the women's movement (62). But she fails to consider that a gender order that aligns males with self-sufficiency and females with passivity deserves at the very least to be disturbed.

What makes gender trouble so suitable for the horror genre is its commitment to transgressing boundaries. Horror blurs boundaries and mixes social categories that are usually regarded as discrete, including masculinity and femininity. Thus, the surviving female is coded ambiguously, as "feminine" through her function as object of aggression and "abject terror personified," and as "masculine" through her exercise of the controlling gaze and ability to use violence. Moreover, the slasher film breaks down binary notions of gender narratively and stylistically. Narratively, women use violence against men effectively; men are symbolically castrated. Stylistically, women exercise the controlling gaze; men function as objects of aggression. Furthermore, the shift in POV shots from the killer to the surviving female promotes cross-gender identification in the audience.

By breaking down binary notions of gender, the horror genre opens up a space for feminist discourse and constructs a subject position for female viewers. What is at stake for the female audience of the slasher film? Consider how the genre violates the taboo against women wielding violence, supplies excessive narrative justification for the surviving female to commit and the audience to enjoy the violence, and puts it in the capable hands of the surviving female who becomes a powerful source of identification and pleasure for female viewers.

. . . And Then She Killed Him

The slasher film violates the taboo against women wielding violence to protect themselves by staging a scene in which she is forced to choose between killing and dying. The starkness of these options is overdetermined. She finds the mutilated dead bodies of her friends strewn about the place. There can be no doubt of the stalker's intention to hunt her down and kill her, nor of his tireless determination to continue until he succeeds. When her attempts to escape prove futile, she makes a last stand in tenacious defense of her own life. Having chosen to live, she is forced to use extreme violence not once but repeatedly against a killer who will not stay dead. Each time he rises from the ground she must renew her attack. But her violence is justified, framed as a form of righteous slaughter.[13] Unlike Erik Menendez, or other high profile killers who turn against their aggressors, she cannot be faulted for not calling for help or for failing to use less extreme measures. The circumstances are such that she cannot be second-guessed. The horror of the universe that calls her violence into play is well-established. The spectacle of the killer's violence narratively motivates her use of extreme force, which the audience cheers. It also functions to mitigate the stigma usually attached to females who use violence and thus encroach on male terrain. The narrative justification for female rage and violence provides what Kirsten Marthe Lentz (1993, 378) calls a "moral alibi" for the fictional woman's violence and the female viewer's pleasure.

The slasher film is an imaginary staging of women who fight back with lethal force against male figures who stalk and try to kill them. Like the female revenge films, such as *Thelma and Louise* of which Lentz (380) writes,[14] the slasher film is a not so subtle expression of male anxiety about feminism and female agency. One expression of this anxiety is that women who exercise agency must pay a heavy price for their freedom, à la Thelma and Louise's suicide pact. But in the slasher film, passive women suffer far greater consequences than those who fight back. The slasher film is after all an expression of male anxiety about female agency in which female agency wins out. Part of the pleasure to be gleaned by female viewers lies in the combination of arousing such anxieties in men while securing female victory.

But what of people, especially women, who report no pleasure, only displeasure, in the violent spectacle of the slasher film? People who find it necessary not only to look away but to keep away from these films often claim that the experience is too frightening, that it makes them feel too vulnerable.[15] I suggest that more than the reported fear of victimization is at stake in this terror, that what motivates the avoidance of this violent genre is not only fear of being victimized but also fear of being violently aggressive. When identification with the agent of violence, especially the monster, becomes too conflictual, the whole setup precludes the construction of recreational terror and teeters the viewer into the realm of terror. But for those viewers who do gain pleasure from indulging in such taboo feelings, the genre provides a cathartic outlet, and in some cases even an expression of feminist feeling.

The slasher film stages a fantasy in which humiliation is transformed into unbridled female rage. The fantasy of female rage is akin to the rape fantasy as feminists have analyzed it[16] (Boston Women's Health Book Collective 1984, 166; Friday 1973, 109; Hite 1976). The female viewer can identify with a female character who has no choice but to use extreme violence against a male killer. Both fantasies enable women to experience taboo emotions (be they rage or sexual arousal) and vicarious actions (be they killing or fucking) without the onus of guilt. As with a rape fantasy, the female viewer is *forced* to vicariously indulge feelings and actions forbidden to her, and although she is "forced" she is in a position to stop it or leave if it does not suit her.

However, as may be evident from the analogy with the rape fantasy, the subject position for women that the slasher film constructs is nonetheless inscribed within the parameters of a male-dominated society, and so there are limits to the agency accorded the woman character or viewer. As Dika (95) observes, when the surviving female kills the killer, she loses narrative agency, i.e., she loses vision, the ability to use violence, and the ability to drive the narrative forward. The killer's death or escape halts the plot but not necessarily the horror; it reinstates the surviving female in the passive position to which female characters are conventionally relegated. In the end, she is caught within the confines of the frame and reinstated as spectacle.

Even more disturbing is that the killer's escape (or resurrection in a subsequent film) implicitly threatens the surviving female with his violent return (Dika 95). This threat can lead to one of various possibilities: another successful outcome for the returning female, as in *Halloween 2* (1981); or it can lead to the death of the surviving female in the sequel, as in *A Nightmare on Elm Street 3: Dream Warriors* in which Nancy dies.[17] A third possibility is found in *Friday the 13th, Part 2* where the surviving female of the preceding film reappears, only to be killed at the outset.

But despite the fact that patriarchal discourse places severe limitations on the subject position accorded woman within film, the slasher film does create an *opening* for feminist discourse by restaging the relationship between women and violence as not only one of danger in which women are the objects of violence but also as a pleasurable one in which women retaliate to become the agents of violence and defeat the aggressors. The surviving female of the slasher film may be victimized, but she is hardly a victim. The slasher film's potential for feminist discourse comes to fruition in *The Stepfather* (1987).

The Stepfather as Feminist Horror Film

The horror film is a genre laden with contradictory elements, some conducive to feminism, others hostile to it. As such, the idea of a feminist horror film poses from the start an uneasy relationship of elements. *The Stepfather* employs the *subversive* generic conventions of the slasher film while it challenges *conservative* ones to advance its feminism. In the tradition of the slasher film, *The Stepfather* locates the active investigative gaze in a female narrative character, Stephanie, who questions male authority, drives the narrative forward, kills in self-defense, and lives to tell the tale. Although not abandoning the terrorization of women, the film resists the convention of showing the ruined female body and instead substitutes the mutilated *male* body as spectacle. The three people killed graphically on screen are men. This departure from the misogynous tendencies of the slasher film form part of a larger pattern, for *The Stepfather* as a feminist film poses a critique of male dominance, specifically the ideology of the nuclear family and the prerogative of male violence. Its horror, like the political of feminist discourse, is domestic, sown within the fertile soil of the traditional nuclear family.

The opening scene is the scene of the crime. The film opens in the aftermath of the slaughter of a woman and her three children by her husband. The camera pans from a peaceful suburban street littered with autumn leaves to the carnage within one of its middle-class homes. The first horror of the film is evoked by the sight of the killer's bloodied image in the mirror. Although his body is intact, editing techniques cut up his body in a series of extreme close-ups as he washes off the blood and assumes a new identity. The former head of the Morrison family calmly walks past dead bodies lying amid overturned furniture in puddles of blood. In the background, the family portrait hangs over the mantlepiece, the mise-en-scène of middle-class family life. He departs in a jovial mood whistling "Camptown Races."

The opening scene establishes the contradiction between the killer's underlying psychotic fury and his exterior placid stability. It juxtaposes chaos and order in the authoritarian personality. This scene renders Stephanie's intense dislike and distrust of her stepfather, Jerry, not only plausible but imperative. Moreover, it exposes the chaos underlying the normative order and provides narrative justification for the female exercise of violence to come. Our knowledge of the stepfather's violence not only informs how we read the events which unfold, it is also essential in validating Stephanie's perspective, which would otherwise seem unduly paranoid given the prevailing "normality" of Jerry's character. Unlike the other characters, Stephanie distrusts Jerry from the start; she sees through his unflagging calmness and affability, regarding it first as phoney and disturbing, then ultimately as pathological.

Our knowledge of the stepfather's violence not only legitimates Stephanie's perspective for the audience, it also literalizes hyperbolic remarks such as Stephanie's expression of trepidation after being expelled from school: "He's going to kill me." This blend of humor and horror turns Jerry's overuse of clichés, such as "let's bury the hatchet," into threats that only viewers recognize. This literalization of speech elicits comic repartee from the audience and actively engages the audience to read the seemingly innocuous as fraught with danger.

The stepfather articulates the conservative ideology of family values invented by Republicans in the eighties as part of a larger antifeminist platform (one founded on a rigid class and race social hierarchy) and underwritten by the recycling and recontextualizing of media artifacts of the late fifties and early sixties.[18] He sees the world through the prism of fifties family sit-coms, those exemplars of the cult of domesticity and the idealized white suburban nuclear family. Indeed, the film makes references to *Mr. Ed, Father Knows Best,* and *Leave It to Beaver.*[19] Jerry models his life on those prefabricated television images of the "good life": Ronald Reagan's America where the benevolent father rules with loving austerity, mother keeps house, and children respect their elders. The film draws a connection between the fifties myth of the family grounded in male authority, and the violent underside of domestic violence. (David Edelstein aptly titled his review in *The Village Voice,* "Ward Wields the Cleaver.") He marries into ready-made families; he spouts sit-com platitudes. Like the television industry he compulsively repeats formulas and ruthlessly cancels failures. Like the Teflon President, Jerry is a consummate chameleon and image salesman. Employed by American Eagle Realty, Jerry unabashedly claims to be selling what he has already bought: The American Dream.

Unlike Jerry, Stephanie's definition of family does not conform to conservative rhetoric. Although she misses her father, she understands that mother and daughter constitute a family. She tells her psychiatrist, Dr. Bondurant, "If he wasn't here, my Mom and I would be alright." She perceives that Jerry's vision is warped. In contrast, Stephanie's mother Susan idealizes Jerry and believes that only with him can they be a "real family" again. At issue here is the question of whose vision is legitimated.

Although Stephanie's perceptions are regarded skeptically by other narrative characters, they are validated for the audience by the structure of the film. Important in this respect is the film's one use of the voice-off, a disembodied voice belonging to a character not visible in the frame, emanating from elsewhere. The film juxtaposes the visual image of Jerry building a birdhouse with the aural image of Stephanie's voice speaking disparagingly about him to her best friend Karen. The film's use of the disembodied female voice corresponds to the film's refusal to accord Jerry the disembodied gaze characteristic of the slasher film. The conventional slasher film positions a man as voyeur and subjects women to more intense scrutinization than men only to overturn these roles when the surviving female subjects the killer to her murderous gaze. *The Stepfather* resists even this initial scrutinization of women. In a notable departure, neither the unclaimed point-of-view shot nor the solitary reaction shot, which establish the dominance of the male gaze, are used in the film. These moves diminish his control while enhancing her authority.

Undaunted by their doubts, Stephanie turns her gaze to the task of investigating Jerry's undisclosed past. An opportunity arises when an article appears in the newspaper about the still-at-large mass murderer of the Morrison family. Ever faithful to patriarchal prerogatives, Jerry ponders with dismay that a man could be "driven" to murder by his family. And why? He tells us, because they disappointed him. At which point, Jerry looks menacingly at Stephanie and the camera cuts to her watching him. His plastic features shift from innocuousness to rage, then back to a warm smile that leaves the viewer cold. This image reverberates with the double meaning of the name of the town in which the Morrison murders took place: Bellevue, beautiful view and site of insanity. The attractive façade hides internal derangement.

In the conventional slasher film, when the killer infiltrates normal society his identity is hidden from the audience. In contrast, Jerry's identity is hidden only from the story's characters. Stephanie's suspicions about his "creepiness" are bolstered when she inadvertently witnesses Jerry's rant in the basement workshop, Jerry's private getaway. In a litany of abuses toward "Daddy's little boy," which culminates in an enraged assertion of the sanctity of the family, he displays the sustained warfare that rages inside him. Disjointed voices alternate between despair, volatile endearments, rage, and calls for order. Badly frightened by this display, Stephanie escalates her scrutiny by writing to the paper for a photograph of Henry Morrison.

As a male psychiatrist, Dr. Bondurant occupies a position of authority within the narrative. As the voice of male rationality, he disputes her ostensibly excessive assessments of Jerry's behavior. Bondurant rationalizes the outburst that she witnesses as a normal form of letting off steam. Although he discredits Stephanie's belief that Jerry is crazy, his concern deepens when she confides that Jerry frightens her. Intent on scrutinizing Jerry even after Jerry refuses to meet with him, Bondurant devises a plan. Posing as a prospective house buyer, a "confirmed bachelor" who disparages "the family, home sweet home, and all that crap," Bondurant provokes Jerry. Calling him a "cheerleader for the traditional family," he interrogates Jerry about his strict upbringing. But disarmed by Jerry's easy manner, Bondurant slips and mentions his wife, bringing to a boil Jerry's suspicions. Jerry seizes a two-by-four and beats him to death.

True to the conventions of the horror genre, the rational skeptic, usually a man, dies. Bondurant's reliance on his ability to manage the encounter with professional expertise leaves him unprepared for the suddenness and ferocity of the attack. Unable to believe in Jerry's murderous violence, he is unprepared to defend himself. In an inversion of the convention that graphically depicts female death far in excess of male death, *his* exercise of an active investigating gaze is punished in a protracted, graphic sequence. Bondurant screams and jerks spasmodically as Jerry hammers at his body. The beam bisects the frame in a relentless rhythm. The voice of male rationality is stilled by the madman who in his madness calls for order. Bondurant's belated ability to see is inscribed in the look of horror in his dead eyes.

Although Jerry has sabotaged Stephanie's investigation of his past by intercepting the photograph sent by the newspaper and replacing it, the film reasserts the clarity of Stephanie's vision even as she doubts herself. It crosscuts between Stephanie telling her friend Karen that she was completely wrong about her stepfather and Jerry disposing of Bondurant's body by staging a car accident. Shorn of her suspicions, Stephanie responds to the news of Bondurant's death by crying in Jerry's arms. Having blocked her vision, Jerry disarms her and opportunistically steps into the vacant space left by the loss of another father figure. It is then that Stephanie makes conciliatory gestures toward Jerry and helps him erect the birdhouse, which symbolizes his vision of the family. But this accord is short-lived.

Jerry's response to Stephanie's sexual agency precipitates the argument that carries him to the point of no return. When she and her friend Paul kiss goodnight, Jerry bursts through the door and, in terms which reveal his sexual disgust, accuses Paul of rape. Disavowing the sexual agency that Stephanie unambiguously expresses, he claims that "she's not ready for this." Paul is guilty of imposing his desire because Stephanie supposedly has no desire of her own. In anger, Stephanie retaliates by calling him crazy, demented, and hung up on sex. This verbal attack marks her ability to see through him again, asserts her sexual agency, and restores her willingness to undermine his authority. Stephanie's refusal to conform to Jerry's antisexual dictums establishes that this surviving female is not a sexual loner. Her desire threatens Jerry because it lies beyond his control. He attempts to stifle her sexuality because he cannot allow her to become autonomous and leave the nest. Jerry's definition of family requires children who are the property of their father. As a teenager, in a liminal state between childhood and adulthood, Stephanie is bound to upset Jerry's need for a strictly ordered world.

The Thanksgiving dinner that precedes the argument epitomizes Jerry's fleeting realization of ideal family life. It is picture-perfect yet full of references to impending disaster. Jerry evokes his status as patriarch when he gives thanks to the Father. But biblical fathers demand sacrifices, and often the sacrificial lamb is the offspring. It is Stephanie's refusal to be controlled by a domineering male that leads to Jerry's decision to kill again.

Their fight sets the stage for Jerry's murderous rampage. The violent climax departs from the generic conventions of the slasher film in a radically significant way; it stages the protracted murder of a domestic psychopath by *two women acting in concert*. The struggle begins when Susan confronts Jerry with the knowledge that he surreptitiously quit his job, a fact he denies. Just as he is convincingly explaining away this "misunderstanding" he slips into his new identity and calls himself "Bill Hodgkins" and mutters "Who am I here?" Having committed this irrevocable slip, he bludgeons Susan with the phone. After beating and kicking her down the basement stairs, Jerry climbs toward the bathroom, where Stephanie is showering, intent on stabbing her to death. Stephanie's shower scene is a reference to *Psycho* that elevates the audience's anxiety level.

Jerry's assault on Stephanie is temporarily delayed by the arrival of his former brother-in-law who has tracked him down, and who like Bondurant before him, underestimates Jerry and pays with his life. His demise obliterates the possibility of rescue by a hero. Having disposed of him, Jerry goes after Stephanie. When Jerry lunges at Stephanie with a knife, she whips it out of her way with a towel and locks herself in the bathroom. Jerry batters the bathroom door and shatters the mirror. In the tradition of the female survivor, Stephanie uses a towel to fashion a shard of glass into a makeshift knife. When Jerry breaks through the door she stabs him in the arm and runs to the attic. Giving chase, Jerry falls through the insulation to the bathroom beneath. Stephanie climbs down and sees her battered mother on the staircase landing below. Susan shouts a warning as Jerry charges, knocking Stephanie to the floor. Susan shoots Jerry but he renews his attack against Stephanie. She calls to Stephanie to get the knife. Stephanie wrests the knife away from him and stabs him in the chest. The reception this sequence received when I saw the film in theatrical release in Manhattan and when I screened it for students at the State University of New York at Purchase was one of vociferous, passionate approval ("shoot him again," "kill him"), especially from the female members of the audience.

The last shot of this sequence, which follows Jerry's death, shows Stephanie looking stunned and exhausted. In the tradition of the slasher film, the image of the woman "trapped within the confines of the frame and returned to her position as object," is one of the last images of the film (Dika 95). Once the female survivor has vanquished the killer, she loses her motivation for vision and violence, and thus loses her ability to drive the narrative forward. But *The Stepfather* subverts this usurpation of female agency with the epilogue.

In the final scene, it is spring and Susan's injuries have healed. Stephanie uses a power saw to cut down the birdhouse,

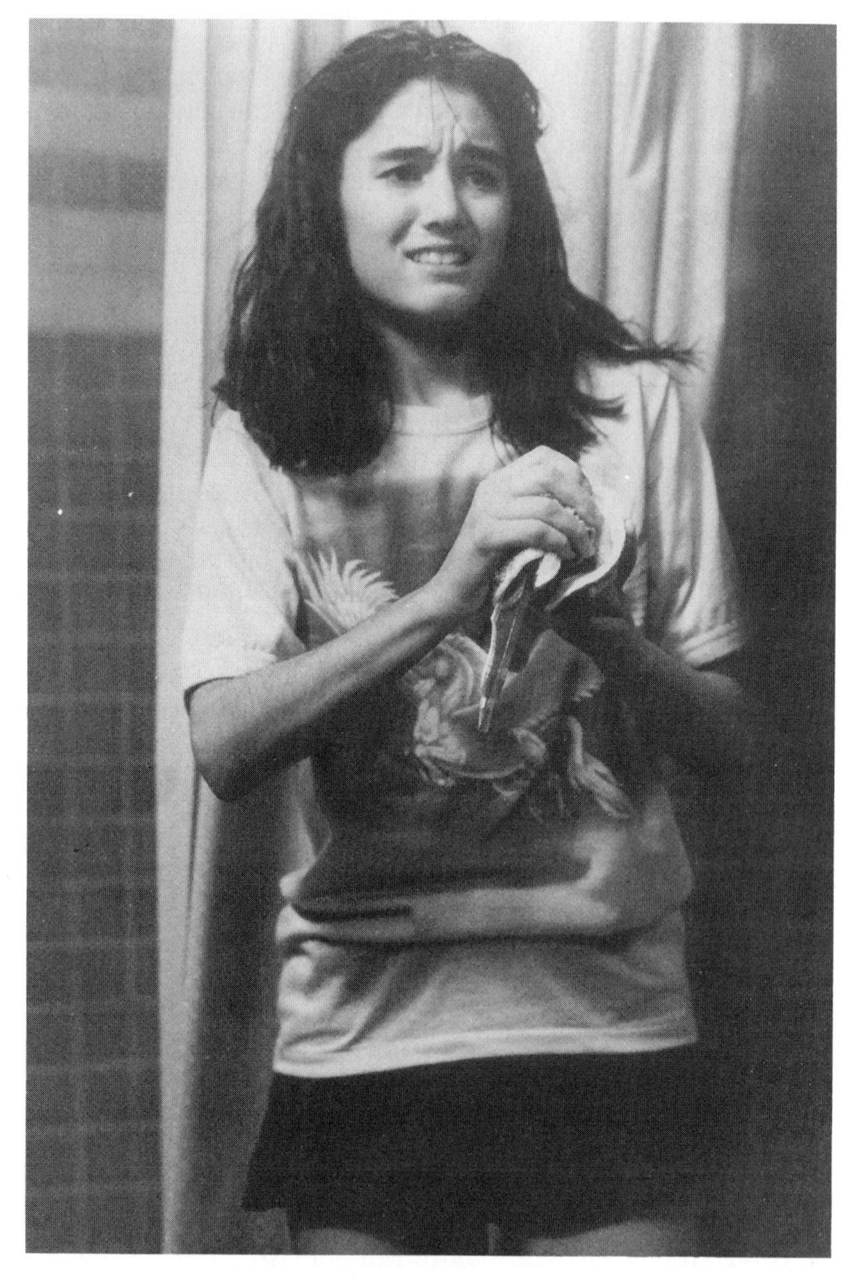

FIGURE 3.3. In the tradition of the female survivor, Stephanie uses a towel to fashion a shard of glass into a makeshift knife in *The Stepfather* (1987). Courtesy of Museum of Modern Art Film Stills Archive.

Jerry's totem to the patriarchal family, as her mother looks on. The pole tumbles in a figurative castration. Mother and daughter embrace and walk into the house as the shattered figure of the birdhouse looms in the foreground. The film's closed ending forecloses the threat of the killer's imminent return so common in conventional slasher films.[20] The two women survive to reconstitute a family, one which allows for female agency. *The Stepfather*, an exemplary instance of that strange hybrid, the feminist horror film, answers Teresa DeLauretis's (1984, 67–68) call that a feminist film create a space for the female subject without abandoning narrative and visual pleasure.

The horror film speaks both *to* women and *about* them, often by articulating the legitimacy of female rage in the face of male aggression and by providing forms of pleasure for female viewers. *The Stepfather* comes closer to realizing the subversive potential of the genre than most others. The film takes to its logical extreme the male dominance championed by the conservative discourse of family values in which men control women's bodies and determine the course of women's lives. And it does so in ways that activate the myriad pleasure-producing dynamics of recreational terror. It is important to remember that the success of a political movement depends not only on analyzing women's oppression but also on mobilizing women's pleasure (Lentz 1993, 398). This double movement comes to fruition in *The Stepfather*. While not explicitly advocating widespread social change, the film does offer a *politics of direct action* in which women join forces to fight back in self-defense and win.

CHAPTER FOUR

The Cultural Politics of the Postmodern Horror Film

Not all postmodern horror films bring to fruition the feminist potential of the genre. But that is not to say that they are otherwise without progressive potential as I will show with *Henry: Portrait of a Serial Killer*. A film like *Henry*, which pushes the boundary between representation and real violence, provides an opportunity to explore the debates that surround the question of violence in film from a leftist perspective.

Henry: Portrait of a Serial Killer

"He's not Freddy. He's not Jason. He's real."

—promotional slogan for *Henry*

Henry: Portrait of a Serial Killer, like so many other postmodern horror films, draws a universe in which normality and abnormality, good and evil become virtually indistinguishable. But unlike other horror films, it earned an unconditional *X* rating from the Motion Picture Association of America (MPAA). Ordinarily, when the MPAA issues an *X* it also stipulates changes that can be made to merit the more box-office-friendly *R* rating. But in *Henry*'s case, no such stipulations were offered. The problem with the film was its overall "disturbing moral tone" (McDonough 1990, 59). What boundaries did the film transgress to warrant this condemnation? Produced in 1986, but not widely released until 1990, it sat on the distributor's shelf for years, largely because it failed to conform to the more conventional features of the postmodern horror film. Released unrated, the controversial film provoked both vitriolic comments ("It's disgusting exploitation." [Pollack 1990, 3F]) and critical acclaim (it made some film critics' 1990 top-ten list). The film invokes the slasher subgenre in both its title and advertising campaign, which draws comparisons to the monsters of *A Nightmare on Elm Street* ("He's not Freddy") and *Friday the 13th* ("He's not Jason"). Although the film is more a deviation from the genre than a typical example, it is precisely these deviations that shed light on the more conventional products.

Henry details the sanguinary activities of a psychotic serial killer who appears normal, at times even likeable. He is clearly the narrative center, the subject of a portrait whose face implies a Cartesian subject but which ultimately masks a deeply divided self whose violence ruptures any semblance of normality. In this film, it is normality that masks the killer whose promised portrait grows murkier as the film develops.

In a conversation with his ex-con roommate, Henry talks about the routine and necessary character of killing, an act he commits with neither glee nor remorse.

HENRY: *You telling me you never killed anybody before?*
OTIS: *I ain't saying that.*
HENRY: *Then you killed before, right?*
OTIS: *Well maybe I didn't have no choice.*
HENRY: *You didn't have no choice here neither. Did you? . . . It's always the same and it's always different. . . . Open your eyes, Otis. Look at the world. It's either you or them. You know what I mean.*
OTIS: *Yeah.*
HENRY: *Good. You want a beer?*

This exchange takes place shortly before Henry initiates Otis into recreational murder, schooling him in the importance of varying murder weapon and location to elude capture. For Henry the act of killing is ordinary, incidental to everything else that he does, important but no more so than having to eat. The routine character of Henry's violence is never explained, but unlike the violence of other monsters, it is couched in the context of a larger life.

Although unambiguously human, Henry is unwavering in his obsession and profoundly immune to appeals for mercy. He strikes without warning and picks his victims seemingly at random, thus rendering everyone a potential victim, although as with most serial killers his victims are predominantly female. The film's advertising discourse ("He's real") directed expectations by drawing authenticating claims to "real-life serial killer" Henry Lee Lucas as the basis for the film. Similarly, film reviews almost invariably allude to this source. These extratextual claims to reality coupled with the documentary feel of the film lend it a "real-life" quality. At the dark heart of this film lies the central force driving the postmodern genre: the constant threat of inexplicable violence aimed at the body. The film's striking sense of malevolence is rooted in the real-life manner in which the film constructs this threat.

The opening sequence establishes Henry as the organizing center of the film. In a montage of scenes that juxtapose both the violent and the mundane quality of Henry's life, we are introduced to the unpredictable and ferocious nature of the postmodern universe. The innovative way in which the narrative opens makes it worth discussing in some detail.

The sequence opens with an extreme close-up of a dead face. The camera pulls back in a circular motion to reveal the naked body of a bruised woman with a bloody gash across her abdomen. Her body lies in a grassy field where birds twitter in the background and leaves rustle in the breeze. A musical code overlays the sounds of nature.

Cut to Henry, a polite, soft-spoken young man, eating at a diner.

The camera pans across a liquor store counter to reveal the strewn bodies of a middle-aged couple with bullet holes through their heads. The musical code marks an acoustic flashback: Bullets fire, a woman screams, and a man barks "shut up!" The musical code recedes as a siren wails.

Cut to Henry driving down the highway as he listens to country music.

The camera pans from the bloody sheets on a bed to a blood-splattered bathroom where a woman semidressed in sexy lingerie (garter belt, stockings, high heels) is sitting on the toilet, her hands bound. Her body is bloody, and a broken bottle is planted in the side of her face. The phone rings as water runs in the sink. The musical code signals an acoustic flashback: A woman coos "oooh baby," a man shouts "shut up, shut up," a bottle breaks, screams sound, and a man yells "die bitch . . . die . . . die . . . die."

Cut to Henry driving as he listens to a weather forecast.

The camera tracks a plastic bottle drifting through a waterway past the body of a woman lying face down in her underwear. The sleeve of a red dress hangs on her arm. Water rushes and birds sing. In the acoustic flashback clothing tears, a woman's muffled screams cry out, and a body falls into the water.

The opening sequence establishes the graphic nature of the violence in the film, the film's departure from the conventions of the slasher film, the randomness of the killings, and the unpredictability of the film's postmodern universe.[1] Although the film privileges the act of showing the spectacle of the ruined body, it substitutes not-hearing for not-seeing in the opening sequence. The acoustic flashbacks are muted and distorted echoes of what happened, a muffled tangle of pitiable screams, abusive language, and electronic sounds. As the camera moves around the lifeless bodies, we hear bits and pieces of the soundtrack of the murder, particularly disembodied screams. The temporal disjunction between the present of the visual track and the past of the sound track is unsettling and disorienting. Like the play of light and shadow in the chiaroscuro tradition, the muted sound track simultaneously reveals and withholds the violent encounter. *Henry* brings into play the pleasure of not-hearing. An arrested or blocked acoustic image is juxtaposed with a graphic visual image to play up the dialectic between the pleasure of seeing (more fully) and the pleasure of not (fully) hearing. The unpredictability of the film set up by the opening sequence means that from the start, the outcome is always in question.

After the opening sequence, Henry's car pulls into the parking lot of a shopping mall. Seemingly at random, Henry picks out a lone woman and follows her home. Both the editing of the opening sequence and the title connect him to the murders, and from this we can impute his motive for following the woman. Henry is on the prowl for his next victim. When he later returns to the house we do not see the murder, only its aftermath. The camera pans from the back of the woman's head to a full frontal shot. Her neck is wrapped with phone wire. The straps of her camisole hang off her shoulders. Her chest and face are branded with cigarette burns. Her neck is discolored with bruises. In the acoustic flashback we hear a sound crash, a woman screams and gasps for breath as she chokes. Once again, the film juxtaposes the ruined body with the muted and distorted acoustic flashback of the murder.

The killer's body is conspicuously missing from the scenes of death, not because of subjective camera work like the unclaimed POV shot or the solitary reaction shot which the film eschews, but because Henry is no longer on the scene when we see the dead bodies. In contrast to the conventional slasher film, most of the murders take place off-screen, and the most graphic on-screen murders are of men.[2] Given the degree to which the film withholds the image of Henry during the act of killing, it is interesting to note the scenes in which we do see Henry murder. The first involves two prostitutes and is cloaked in shadows. Two others, extended murders that occur in close range and in graphic detail, involve unseemly, unlikable male characters (the fence and Otis). But one particular set of on-screen murders stands out. This is the scene reviewers characterize in hyperbolic tones as "the film's strongest, hardest-to-sit-through sequence" (Newman 1991, 44); "the grisliest episode" (Arnold 1990, E1); "the most piteous and appalling sequence in memory" (Benson 1990, F1). Indeed, the strong reactions the film elicited led Caryn James of the *New York Times* to make overdrawn claims about the violence depicted in the film. In tones reminiscent of *The Wizard of Gore*, the woman with the gash across her abdomen became "one woman practically sawed in half" (1990, C12).

The sequence in question opens with Henry and Otis prowling a suburb by car as the electronic score that signifies

Henry's violence in the flashbacks plays. We see the torture-murder of a suburban nuclear family unfold within the frame of a camcorder: Otis walks into the frame restraining a woman's arms from behind. Her struggles and gagged screams are a constant throughout most of the scene. A man's reflection is visible in the mirror behind them, the reflection of Henry holding the videocamera. We hear Henry say, "Bring her in Otis. . . . Get her blouse off." As Henry prods and encourages: "Take it off . . . oh yeah Otis," Otis gropes her body. "Do it Otis." The camera pans to a bloodied man semi-conscious on the ground, tied, and blindfolded, a towel jammed into his mouth. He is moaning and moving feebly. Henry kicks him and yells, "shut up," an echo of the voice in the acoustic flashbacks heard at the opening of the film. The adolescent son unexpectedly walks through the front door. As he takes in the scope of the danger, the camera falls to the floor at an oblique angle. Henry enters the frame and lunges at the fleeing boy. They grapple until Henry breaks the boy's neck. In solidarity, Otis snaps the woman's neck. Henry takes out a switchblade and steps off-screen to where the man is bound and gagged. We can hear the knife stabbing, and the man's death throes as we see Otis kiss and fondle the dead woman. Henry picks up the camera and pans across the bleeding and broken bodies. Otis toys with the dead woman's arm waving it in mock gesture. He pulls down her pantyhose to violate her corpse but stops when Henry vehemently yells no.

Cut to Henry and Otis watching the snuff videotape on television much as we the audience have been watching *Henry*.[3] This three-minute scene shot cinéma-verité style, without editing, and in long shot, produces an intense documentary realism that noticeably disturbed reviewers and other audience members. As Hal Hinson reports, "it's hard to know how to react . . . we feel as if we've been drawn into something we didn't quite expect; as if, unwittingly, we've become accomplices in the making of a snuff film" (1990, D7). Similarly, Eleanor Ringel declares, "Then, when we've pretty much let down our guard, the filmmaker smacks us in the face with one of the most shocking sequences I've ever seen on film" (1990, D5). The impact of the torture-murder is intensified when we realize that it is constructed largely around what we cannot see until the scene cuts to the killers, only to have Otis insist on watching the video again in slow motion. What appeared to be a live event unfolding in real time is revealed to be merely a tape of a live event, a record of the murders seen in the aftermath of the crime. What seemed to be a scene in which the audience stands apart from the killers and looks in voyeuristically at their deeds is shown to be one in which the audience watches the videotape in the company of the killers. The audience is gulled and unwittingly implicated in a compromising manner in voyeurism.

Although this scene invariably generated strong reactions from critics, missing from film reviews is an admission of the sexually provocative nature of the scene, or the sense in which the video simulates snuff by combining the pornographic with murder. I discussed this film with four women (all feminists, two heterosexual, two lesbian) who acknowledged feeling sexually aroused during this scene and then being taken aback by their own responses. Although this reaction is not generalizable to all viewers, the fact that some female viewers experienced this tangle of emotions does suggest one possible reading strategy deployed by women in the audience.[4] One viewer I spoke to summarized well the ambivalent quality of the experience:

> My reaction to the scene was really uncomfortable because it is a very scary scene, really brutal. But for some reason while they're basically torturing this woman before killing her, I felt sexually aroused. I am not usually turned on by depictions of rape or men abusing women, but for some reason I had this very weird physical response, which I still can't account for.[5]

Howie Movshovitz of the *Denver Post* comes close to recognizing this reaction when he relates that after the torture-murder of the family: "The movie's killing and violence lose their attraction and there's a sense of shame, as if someone caught you watching something dirty" (1990, 7). This scene is so disturbing because it structures an identification with the killers, one that takes viewers by surprise. As another viewer reported: "Before I realized it, I was feeling a mixture of horror and sexual arousal during this scene. This was disturbing as I realized I was experiencing what the killers were experiencing."[6] This viewer voices the dismay many viewers, including critics, expressed over being implicated in the violence, placed in an untenable position, unsettled by the realization of complicity. I suspect this scene's combination of sexual excitement and fear played a pivotal role in the MPAA's condemnation of the film's "disturbing moral tone" as well as in their refusal to specify their objections.

The film leaves unanswered the question of why Henry kills. Aside from the conversation with Otis in which Henry flatly asserts the inevitability of violence ("It's either you or them"), the film stages a conversation between Henry and Becky, Otis's sister, with whom he briefly shares memories of childhood sexual abuse and violence. But the glib manner in which he recounts this tabloid history together with his capacity to forget just how he killed his abusive mother (bludgeoned, stabbed, or shot) produces an incoherent account. Henry's minimal self-narrative is not even remotely adequate to the task. He is unable to explain himself. All we are left with is the impression that Henry is irreparably damaged. His compulsion to kill is impersonal and follows its own inexorable, but unmapped, course.

Henry's murderous partnership with Otis crumbles when Henry discovers Otis raping Becky. He intervenes to protect her and with Becky's help (she stabs Otis in the eye with a steel comb), he kills Otis. The two leave town together after disposing of the body. They stop for the night at a motel. The next morning Henry drives off alone. He pulls off to the side of the road, takes Becky's suitcase out of the trunk and dumps the bloody bag. The only trace of Becky's murder is a brief acoustic flashback of screams as Henry hoists the suitcase. Becky never learns about Henry's killing spree. Her warm feelings for him grant her no immunity from his violence. There is no protracted struggle from which she or anyone else emerges a survivor. Henry remains an enigma. The portrait that promises depth, a glimpse into the soul, delivers a bland surface beneath which lurks a soulless monster.

At the end of the film Henry is a predator at large, an unambiguously human psychotic, mortal but undefeated. The film staunchly refuses to condemn, punish, or explain Henry. It ends the way it opens, flouting the conventions of the slasher film. The apocalyptic impulse of the film leaves its most sympathetic character dead, dumped unceremoniously by the side of the road, and its central character an unredeemable predator loose in the world. The flat inevitability of violence in the film works not to neutralize the violence but rather to raise the audience's anxiety level. It constitutes a highly charged deviation from the generic norm that leaves the audience constantly guessing what direction this unconventional ride will take next. *Henry* demonstrates the central lesson of the postmodern horror genre: that cloaked in a mantle of normalcy, chaos lies just beneath the surface ready to erupt at any moment.

The Question of Violence

The portrait *Henry* paints is dimly lit and out of focus. But neither Henry's enigmatic identity nor the genre's apocalyptic impulse compels us to accept at face value the postmodern horror film's construction of violence as inevitable and inexplicable. To define violence as enigmatic is to erase the social grounds that determine whether violence flourishes or withers, as well as the varieties of violence which prevail.[7] But the horror film's purpose is not to explain violence; it is to stage the terror and rage of a postmodern society.

Serial killers and related figures like Jason or Freddy embody chaotic destructive forces that, from the perspective of everyday life, strike seemingly at random.[8] But upon closer sociological inspection, we can see that threats like terrorism or street violence are the products of complex social factors, such as the religious ideology which fuels antiabortion terrorism or the proliferation of guns used in street violence to lethal effect, a proliferation promoted by the National Rifle Association whose campaign contributions allow it to exert undue influence in Congress. What horror films do best is to capture the experience of helplessness that results when violence is wrest from its social grounds, and we are left looking for explanations solely at the psychological level, which yields the category of the psychopath, or at the behavioral level, which produces the argument that the mass media itself precipitates violence.

At its narrowest, the behavioral model argues that viewers of horror films imitate depicted violence. At its broadest, it argues that the violent horror film promotes a cultural milieu hostile to women. But if it is true that filmic violence precipitates real-life violence, then the horror film at least deserves some credit for precipitating female self-defense. However, I am unconvinced that popular culture can be credited with this power, or saddled with primary responsibility for violent acts in society.

The power of the single-bullet theory that violence in the media causes violence in everyday life is that it is able to direct anger and fear about real-life atrocities into a concrete and emotionally satisfying target. Simplistic though it may be, this argument appeals because it lends itself to scapegoating and thus to the tunnel vision that allows its adherents to ignore the complex web of institutionalized social relations which underlie violence in society. Attacks against violence on film and in other media not only displace attention from the underlying social causes of violence onto visible forms of controversial entertainment but also provide a condensed and comforting explanation for social problems that are in actuality vastly more difficult to address than this discourse would have us believe. To accord horror films the power of inducing real-life violence is to make film bear the blame for the larger social processes in which film participates as only one of many factors, while letting larger political and economic practices off the hook.

But rejecting the scapegoating thesis still leaves the question of the political valence of the postmodern horror film. Does it subvert or reinforce the hegemonic order? I have already suggested that it does both, but I would like to consider the question at greater length. Having rejected the position that male viewers simply imitate depicted violence while female viewers cower in terror, or that horror films merely stage an unmitigated attack upon the female body and thereby reinforce a misogynous social order, it is still possible to conceive of the horror film as a bad cultural object. To the extent that horror films reinforce the ideology of the individual—in the "intimate apocalypse" the attack is launched against the individual body, the surviving female usually takes on the killer one-on-one and ends up being the lone survivor—they participate in the flood of cultural representations which discourage collective action and thus defuse progressive political movements. Moreover, the cathartic release the films provide appease viewer frustrations and vitiate the need for social change. Thus entertainment displaces politics.

This, however, is not the only possible outcome. The cathartic release horror affords may also empower viewers to engage in other activities, including progressive political action, if they are so inclined. Lawrence Grossberg (1988, 170) distinguishes between two forms of empowerment, both of which are at work in the reception of horror. Positive empowerment is celebratory and enabling even though it ignores relations of domination. *The Thing* (1981), with its exemplary dramatization of the postmodern universe, its high level of suspense and spectacular body horror, is likely to produce positive empowerment. In contrast, negative empowerment is critical of and resistant to relations of domination. *The Stepfather* is an example of a horror film that, more explicitly than most, constructs a feminist critique of male domination and is likely to produce negative empowerment.

But even if we accept the appeal and prevalence of feminist elements in the slasher film, especially as they are embodied in the character and agency of the surviving female, we cannot fail to notice the antifeminist animosity directed with particular force against the female body. Boss raises this issue, although in connection to the socially conscious work of George Romero and without regard to gender. He notes that "it is difficult to integrate readings of political progressivity with the fantasies of physical degradation and vulnerability" (1986, 18). To this I respond that the attack upon the body is culturally specific. Given the dominance of the individual within American culture, the intimate apocalypse is the most effective way to stage the experience of helplessness. It may not produce an understanding of postmodern society, but it does allow for the expression of terror and rage. The horror film may be a politically incorrect fantasy with its celebration of violence and scrutiny of the ruined body, but is it not the role of fantasy to safely express desires we would not actually act on? This point (as well as the feminist elements of the slasher film) seems to be lost on Jane Caputi who considers the slasher film "soft-core snuff" and "gorenography" (1990; 6, 9), which she defines as the sexualization of violent behavior intended not only to stimulate the viewer but to "endorse and/or recommend the behavior" (12). Why must this follow? What seems to escape many critics including Caputi is that there is no one-to-one correspondence between film violence and violence in everyday life.

But is there a connection between the violent horror film and the treatment of real-life violence as entertainment? The fascination with bodily ruination that excludes concern for the suffering of the victim was in ample evidence in the coverage of the murders of Nicole Brown Simpson and Ronald Goldman. In the summer of 1994, both the site of the double homicide and the home of alleged killer O. J. Simpson became tourist attractions to rival Disneyland, complete with souvenir hawkers, food vendors, and snapshot takers. What fictional and real-life violence have in common is their location within a capitalist production context that commodifies everything, including death. Critics who take aim at film violence, from mainstream politicians like Senator Bob Dole to the rightwing American Family Association, are loathe to criticize the larger context of capitalism's profit-driven, anything-goes stance and reserve their venom for the Hollywood establishment whose support for a liberal social agenda is anathema to conservatives. Thus, in the culture wars, attacks against the mass media are framed narrowly enough to exclude the larger capitalist framework. What we are left with is a limited critical outcry against the excesses of the genre.

Critical Outcry

The horror film stages the threat of violence and the spectacle of the creative death. Its power to shock is based on the genre's violation of taboos. But when violations become conventionalized through repetition, their violatory nature is neutralized and they are no longer violations in the same sense of the word. For instance, the open-ending and body horror that shocked audiences when *Night of the Living Dead* was released in 1968 no longer have the same power to shock. The process of neutralization produces the ongoing need to revitalize the genre by renaming the taboo element, by violating differently. At different points in the history of the genre, the genre innovates or introduces a new form of violation. What ensues is outrage. Think of the critical outcries to *The Curse of Frankenstein* in 1957, *The Texas Chain Saw Massacre* in 1973, or *Friday the 13th* in 1980. Innovative films are accused of going too far, of being too violent. Old arguments are resurrected, burnished, and presented as new. In each succeeding period those films that came before become the more conventionalized, domesticated forms that have to make way for the newly transgressive incarnation of the genre under attack. The irony is that those who are critical of the violence in the current genre consider earlier forms of the genre innocuous despite the outrage they too elicited at an earlier time.

The success of the horror genre lies in its capacity to transgress, so calling forth a critical outcry becomes a test of the genre's effectiveness. Each passing phase of the genre has but a momentary capacity to outrage. (The slasher film, for instance, has long been highly conventionalized in ways that are very familiar to fan audiences.) *Henry: Portrait of a Serial Killer* is in the rare position of refiguring the violation. This film departs so thoroughly from generic conventions, for instance, through its extension of the pleasures of not-seeing to the pleasures of not-hearing, that the overall effect is a film which constantly unsettles viewer expectations. For those who know the genre, there is an ongoing dissonance between what goes on in the film and the expectations generated by the slasher film, expectations which *Henry*'s advertising strategy sets into motion.

Although I have argued for the progressive potential of the genre, the political valence of each succeeding postmodern horror film cannot be ascertained in advance. That will depend on both the combination of conventions deployed in the film and on how the film is interpreted by fans and critics. Although *Henry* opens up new avenues for the development of the genre in its postmodern vein, its innovations have yet to be adopted by other horror films. *Henry* still occupies the extreme edges of the genre. More abundant are the trite productions that people normally think of when they think of horror, i.e., the prolific films with big box office takes and tiny variations. It will be interesting to see the permutations that the genre takes, for horror is a genuinely resilient genre, one that refuses to die.

The monstrification of race is a permutation of the genre that runs through the history of the contemporary horror film but one that is seldom discussed. The dearth of serious consideration of race horror is symptomatic of the structuring absence of race in most horror film criticism, an issue I hope to redress.

CHAPTER FIVE

Race Horror

Like the foregoing chapters, the recent spate of feminist criticism on the horror film has largely confined itself to considerations of the monster as a gendered Other (e.g., Williams 1984, Dika 1990, Clover 1992, and Creed 1993). In contrast, writers such as Noel Carroll (1984), Lester Friedman (1984), Judith Halberstam (1995), and Rhona Berenstein (1996) have analyzed instances of the monster as a racial or ethnic Other.[1] The latter approach has gotten short shrift in the wake of both the box office and critical popularity of the slasher film, a subgenre that either excludes racial minorities altogether or relegates them to the status of victims, largely undeveloped expendable characters. And although the slasher film's inscription of gender and sexuality makes it ripe for feminist analysis, this alone does not account for the lack of attention accorded race as an analytic term. At least as important in understanding the overriding concern with sex and gender in the horror film is the dominance of psychoanalytic theory in film criticism.[2] The upshot of all these factors is that race, ignored as an analytic category, is a structuring absence of most horror film criticism.

Race is a structuring absence in the milieu of the contemporary horror film where monsters, victims, and heroes are predominantly white, a racially unmarked category. Halberstam suggests that the horror film avoids racially marked characters because in contemporary American culture race is already monstrified or "gothicized," by which she means "transformed into a figure of almost universal loathing who haunts the community and represents its worst fears" (1995, 4,

18). If the racial Other is marked as monster in the larger culture, then to do so in the horror film is to tread too closely to prevailing anxieties. A more coded figure is called for. Carol Clover (135) proposes that this figure is the lower-class Southern redneck. She argues that racial monstrosity is displaced onto the backwoods redneck in city-revenge films such as *I Spit on Your Grave* (1977) and *The Hills Have Eyes* (1977). These films pit savage rednecks against visiting city folks who react to the atrocities committed against them with violent retaliation.[3]

I would agree with Halberstam and Clover's assessment of the place of race in the postmodern horror film in general. However, a small body of horror films explicitly code the monster as a racial Other. What I have found is that horror films which violate this convention of whiteness also violate another convention of the genre: they are usually set in the city rather than the suburban or rural retreat favored by contemporary horror films. To understand the significance of this breach, let us briefly review the conventions of the postmodern horror film.

The postmodern horror film violates the assumption that we live in a predictable world by demonstrating that we live in a minefield, a world in which the ideological construct of safety systematically unravels. The postmodern genre exposes the terror implicit in everyday life by locating it where it is ideologically least expected: a middle-class suburb in *Halloween*, a summer camp in *Friday the 13th*, the countryside in *Night of the Living Dead*. Because it seeks to disrupt everyday life and supplant security with paranoia, the genre locates the monster in an ideologically safe environment: the rural, innocent pastoral realm, or the suburb, the buffer zone removed from, and in opposition to the city, signifier of corruption.[4] Horror films avoid locating monstrosity in the city where violence is, as a matter of public record, a routine element of everyday life.

So what do we make of the patterned concurrence of not one but two genre violations? What does it mean when the genre violates conventions by locating violence in the city, where it is most expected, and furthermore plays openly on prevailing cultural anxieties by marking the monster as a racial Other? To consider these questions I will analyze a small body of urban horror films that feature the monster as a racial Other.

A word is in order here about which films this criteria excludes. Not all horror films that purportedly take place in a city do so (for example, *Friday the 13th Part 8: Jason Takes Manhattan* [1989] is a slasher film largely situated aboard a ship sailing to Manhattan, which bears only a tangential concern with race—the film throws in two gun-toting youths of ambiguous ethnicity).[5] Moreover, not all urban horror films are overtly concerned with race (e.g., *Rosemary's Baby* [1968] is set in Manhattan but features only white principals). Then there are horror films that racialize the monster but are not set in urban locations. Prominent among these is *Night of the Living Dead* (1968) whose racial politics bears discussing.

Night features as hero the sole black character whose race is, remarkably, unremarked upon. Even the narrow-minded character, Harry, calls Ben a "man" rather than a "black man." In "White," Richard Dyer argues that the representation of whiteness, the culturally unmarked racial category, comes more readily into focus in films that feature non-white characters (47). He points out that all the living dead, whose determination to dominate is resolutely resisted by the hero, are white (59). Since the zombies can be destroyed by burning, the film abounds with scenes of fire. Dyer notes that, in particular, images of molotov cocktails allude to news coverage of the black urban uprisings of that period.[6] Indeed, "'fire,' as an image of Black Power's threat to white people had wide currency" (61).

The besieged farmhouse of *Night of the Living Dead* also recalls the scene in *Birth of a Nation* (1915) in which key white characters take refuge in a farmhouse where they are beset by black brute soldiers. But whereas *Birth* exalts the white supremacist "freedom ride" of the Ku Klux Klan that restores white dominance,[7] *Night* denounces white violence, whether it issues from the sheriff's (white) posse or the (white) living dead. Ben is killed by the forces of the state, whose actions are indistinguishable from the rampage of the zombie mob. At the end of *Night*, Ben's body is unceremoniously burned in a bonfire, the film's last image of fire, one that suggests the Klan's use of fire to rule by terror.[8]

Like *Night of the Living Dead, The Serpent and the Rainbow* (1987) racializes the monstrous and locates it in a rural setting. But unlike *Night*, *Serpent* explores not the savagery of white racists but of black Haitians. A film that ascribes zombieism to voodoo, *Serpent* restores the religious context to zombie films that *Night* so diligently avoids. The white protagonist is an American anthropologist, Dr. Dennis Allen, a scientist who intuitively senses a "dark presence" when in the vicinity of evil. The film associates the political tyranny of the Duvalier regime with voodoo, identified as a religion that can turn dissidents into zombies and use them to terrorize others. Portrayed as a magical religion, voodoo is shown to create profound effects on the body. As the anthropologist's native informant, Marielle, tells him, "Our God is not just in his heaven. He's in our bodies, our flesh." And that flesh is predominantly black. *The Serpent and the Rainbow* associates evil with a darkness of the soul, and disturbingly, with a darkness of the skin.

One film that racializes the monster as white, and that draws on the social conditions of the inner city ghetto, is not included in my group of race horror films because it unfolds not within an urban environment, but inside a large house. *The People Under the Stairs* (1991) features a thirteen-year-old African American nicknamed Fool, who is anything but. His family is poor and faces eviction by ruthless white landlords who plan to convert the apartments into lucrative condominiums. Desperate for money, Fool is persuaded to help rob the landlords, slumlords who call blacks "niggers," and who not only economically exploit minority ghetto residents, but who also kidnap, imprison, and mutilate white youths, whom they stash in the cellar.[9] By the end of the film, Fool locates the landlords' cache of wealth extracted from the poor, and frees the people under the stairs, who proceed to kill their deranged captors. In *The People Under the Stairs*, the monsters are white, marked as racists, and their victims include members of the black community. Like Ben in *Night of the*

Living Dead, Fool is a member of the exploited group who uses his resourcefulness to resist the white onslaught. But unlike Ben, Fool survives.

One other group of films deserves mention here, films more accurately understood as variants of blaxploitation than of urban horror as I use the term. The list includes *Blacula* (1972), its sequel *Scream, Blacula, Scream* (1973), *Blackenstein* (1973), and *Dr. Black, Mr. Hyde* (1976). Both Blacula films feature a black vampire who preys on black victims in Los Angeles, but the monster is more Dracula-in-blackface than a racial Other. Similarly, *Blackenstein,* also known as *Black Frankenstein,* casts Dr. Stein's monster as a black Vietnam veteran whose amputated arms and legs are restored by the doctor. When the experiment is sabotaged, Blackenstein turns murderous. In *Dr. Black, Mr. Hyde,* also known as *The Watts Monster,* Dr. Henry Pride injects himself with an experimental serum intended to reverse liver damage. The serum transforms him into a white-skinned, blue-eyed killer who goes on the rampage in Watts. Although black characters refer to the killer as "a white dude," he looks more interracial than white, thus casting doubt on the claim that the monster is racialized as white (see Hardy 1986, 311). Though these films feature black monsters, they owe more to the blaxploitation formula than to the urban race horror film.

The monster is most likely to be constituted as a racial Other when the genre locates monstrosity in urban centers—such as New York, Chicago, Los Angeles, or Miami—where racial minorities are concentrated in the de facto system of racial segregation that operates in the United States. In addition, the monster of urban horror is associated with a magical religion. It is to these films that I turn.

DIST*URBANCE*

Although as products of the same genre they share some characteristics, the slasher and race horror subgenres can be distinguished by certain key features. The slasher film is set in a suburban or rural location, ideologically coded as a safe environment, whereas race horror locates violence in the city, a site already ideologically coded as dangerous. Race horror retains its capacity to estrange danger by introducing a dark and ancient religion, one associated with savagery and third-world peoples. Whereas in the slasher film, religion—for instance, the use of crosses or holy water—is either absent or ineffectual, in race horror the power of magical religions is amply demonstrated. The monster of race horror is associated with the religion, be it as a follower or a god. African, Aztec, and American Indian religious lore are invoked to explain the nature of the evil at work in the film.

As in the slasher film, the monstrous power at work in race horror is predicated on the inefficacy of science and conventional rationality. The hero of the story must put aside rational skepticism in order to survive. In the slasher film the hero is likely to be a white female, whereas in race horror the hero is likely to be a white male associated with the police or science, sometimes both as in the police psychiatrist of *The Believers*, one who comes to believe in the efficacy of magic. In contrast with the slasher film, which eschews the expert, in race horror the hero is assisted in coming to believe by consulting books on the occult or an expert informant, usually a university professor who has studied the religion. Similar to the slasher film, in race horror the hero usually triumphs, but the ending is left open for further disruptions of the everyday world.

The Possession of Joel Delaney

A forerunner of race horror is *The Possession of Joel Delaney* (1972), which features a white female protagonist who despite desperate attempts to believe in the occult is unable to, with dire consequences. Norah Benson, an elitist Park Avenue denizen who mistreats her Latina housekeeper, Veronica, berates her brother Joel for living among Puerto Ricans in the East Village. When Joel's girlfriend, Sherry, is murdered, Norah suspects not Joel, whose violent behavior has already landed him in Bellevue, but his best friend Tonio Perez, clearly etched in her mind as "the Puerto Rican." The detective investigating the murder confirms her suspicions when he links Sherry's murder to three prior murders of Puerto Rican women for which Tonio was wanted before he disappeared.

Convinced that Tonio is controlling and entangling her troubled brother in murder, Norah implores Veronica to help her. Recognizing the limits of police work and asserting the Otherness of Puerto Ricans, Norah tells Veronica: "It's just possible that the police can't find out anything about this. It's just possible that the people in my world can't get into your world." Norah is prepared to enter Tonio's world to save her brother. She learns that this is the world of Santería, a syncretic religion that mediates between Catholic and Yoruban belief systems. The Santeristas to whom Veronica sends Norah tell her that Tonio is dead but has possessed Joel. With Norah's reluctant cooperation, they perform an exorcism but warn her that its efficacy rests on her ability to open her mind. When the exorcism fails, Norah abandons the cult.

Convinced that Joel is responsible for Sherry's murder, Norah implores Joel's psychiatrist, who is her friend, to have Joel committed. But Joel kills the psychiatrist, eludes capture, and follows Norah and the kids out to the beach house where he terrorizes them. When the police finally kill Joel, Norah runs to his body, grieving. After she touches him, her face takes on a strange expression suggesting that she has now been possessed.

This film is a forerunner of race horror because it deviates from some key features of the subgenre. Although the monster is racialized, *The Possession of Joel Delaney* treats Santería as a powerful religion that can be put to either good or evil use, thereby painting it as a dangerous, but not a savage, religion.[10] Moreover, the protagonist not only fails to believe but she is also unable to help her brother or, ultimately, herself. A more developed instance of race horror is *The Believers*.

The Believers

The Believers (1987) introduces the suburban Jameson family—Cal, Lisa, and their young son Chris—enjoying their morning routine, a routine that is disrupted by an untimely series of events. First, Cal spills a carton of milk on the kitchen floor. Then, the coffee maker short-circuits. Lisa is electrocuted when she goes to unplug the machine while standing in a puddle of milk. A coincidence of minor mishaps results in an irretrievable loss. The film cuts from Lisa's body shaking from the force of electrocution as her husband and son look on in horror, to the shaking body of a masked African man dancing to a cacophony of drums surrounded by other dancers in the Sudan. A white couple deliver their dying five-year-old son to be sacrificed in a ritual that is calculated to check the drought and cholera killing the tribe. Although we later learn that this scene transpired forty years before the first, the opening sequence establishes the two worlds that are to come into conflict in the film—the secular and the magical—and juxtaposes the irrationality of loss in both worlds.

The tragic loss of the first scene motivates Cal to move from the suburbs to Manhattan, where he works as a police psychiatrist and socializes with Lisa's mentor, anthropologist Kate Maslow and her husband Dennis. The two worlds converge when Cal is called upon to counsel Tom Lopez, an undercover cop investigating the disappearance of boys whose mutilated bodies are found ritually arranged on an altar, the fate that befell the boy in the second scene. Lopez is convinced of the efficacy of the sacrificial ritual, a belief Cal relegates to "superstitious nonsense."

The Believers refers to two groups of religious adherents practicing in New York City. The first is a group of working-class Latinos who practice Santería. In the film, Santería is represented largely through the figure of Carmen Ruiz, the Latina housekeeper/nanny who casts a love spell on Cal and his landlady Jessica, and who endeavors unsuccessfully to protect the Jamesons through rituals. The second group of believers is a largely white, upper or upper-middle class coterie of spiritualists who look to an unnamed African for leadership. The African is introduced to the States through Kate and Dennis Maslow, white Columbia University anthropologists who meet him "in the bush" when he is a child. Unlike their dying son who is sacrificed in the opening sequence, the "special boy," now a man, survives the drought. Lacking the mediation of mestizo Latinos and Christianized Santería, the African spiritualists are marked as adherents of a Lovecraftian dark and ancient religion.

The Believers invokes the racist specter of the mesmeric outsider who infiltrates white society with his dark and ancient "god of destruction and pestilence." Both groups of believers are attributed with magical powers, though the unadulterated African spiritualists clearly wield superior power. Both operate from an instrumental system of exchange whereby clearly defined methods are used to produce predictable outcomes; they perform prescribed sacrificial rituals to achieve desired ends. But the stakes with which they operate are vastly different. The Santeristas sacrifice chickens and cats to propitiate divine forces, whereas the spiritualists sacrifice three first-born sons to gain power and destroy their enemies. The efficacy of magic provides the latter with, what one character calls, "a life without uncertainty, freedom from doubt."

Magic—or more to the point, black magic—operates as a critical signifier of racially specific power and racially specific evil. Anthropologist Michael Taussig (1987) argues that the attribution of magical powers to oppressed peoples of color is a colonial construct.[11] Though shamanism predates European colonization, historically it developed in relation to white imperialist power. According to Taussig, from the point of European colonization on, "magic became a gathering point for Otherness in a series of racial and class differentiations embedded in the distinctions made between Church and magic, and science and magic" (465). In other words, the colonial construction of magic aligns white colonial power with civilization and nonwhite colonized people with savagery. This conjunction is borne out in *The Believers*.

For most of the film, blacks are seldom present without the cacophony of drums in the background, signifier of another colonial construct—"native." The first black characters introduced are Sudanese sacrificing a white boy to propitiate the gods. Later, black men drum in Central Park, near the site where the bloodied remains of a Santería sacrifice are found. In

FIGURE 5.1. The African spiritualist and his white acolytes are marked as adherents of a dark and ancient religion in *The Believers* (1987). Courtesy of Museum of Modern Art Film Stills Archive.

narrative dialogue the African foundation of Santería is designated as being a thousand years older than Christianity, brought over by African slaves, thus establishing the exotic and ancient nature of the religion, and its connection to a contest of power. As a mulatto religion, Santería is identified as more African than Catholic, more black than white. But Santería is distinguished from the exotic, more expressly African spiritualism, redeemed by its association with Catholicism. Thus, when a boy is found ritually murdered on an altar in Spanish Harlem, Santería is suspected, but it is *brujería*, "witchcraft," later called "black magic," which is at work.

In his study of the Azande of Central Africa, anthropologist Evans-Pritchard (1976) formulated the relationship between witchcraft and knowledge as "witchcraft explains coincidence," a statement with which the disbelieving Cal, a lapsed Catholic, would agree. But during the course of the film, the power of black magic is amply demonstrated. Police investigators who threaten to expose the murderous activities of the spiritualists are cursed. The first is police detective Lopez, a Santerista who believes in and fears their power. He tells Cal: "They get right inside your body; you can't stop them." They invade your body without your knowledge and thus violate any semblance of security. Lopez dies when he plunges a knife into his abdomen to stop the pain of writhing snakes inside his body, snakes which the autopsy produces as visible evidence of witchcraft.

Magic is directed at the body, which becomes the site of invasion and the locus of anxiety. But the body is a gender-specific body. Lopez is impregnated with phallic snakes and dies when he disembowels himself. When Jessica investigates the spiritualists, she too becomes the target of black magic. A sore develops on her face, which subsequently reddens, festers, and expands to cover most of her cheek. Horrified at the sight of her own body, she retreats into seclusion. The sore eventually throbs and ruptures to release spiders which crawl out and over her deteriorating body. Jessica is impregnated in a less intrusive manner than Lopez but barely survives.

The scenes of invasive pregnancy are ripe with meaning, both for the fears the larger film plays with and for the ending.

For the larger film, they suggest that monstrous, underground, black forces that lurk beneath the surface of society likewise threaten to erupt and overrun the social body. Indeed, the film is littered with references to infiltration and contamination. From Cal, whose job is to uncover buried emotions, to Lopez the undercover cop who insinuates his way into the clandestine circle of believers, infiltration is a constituent part of modern life. But society is also permeated with veiled sinister forces, from Santería's "African gods hidden in Catholic saints" to the conspiratorial underground believers whose reach extends to the upper echelons of corporate power.

By the end of the film, the African is dead, his congregation disabled, and normality ostensibly restored. Cal and Jessica are married, living with Chris in the countryside, and Jessica is pregnant. But previous scenes of invasion beg the question—What is growing inside her?—and the suggestion of a happy ending is quickly aborted. Pregnant, her body once more the locus of anxiety, Jessica has erected a Santerista altar draped with a virtual bestiary of animal sacrifices for protection. When Cal discovers it, she murmurs, "We'll be safe now." The frame freezes on Cal's stricken expression. Unwittingly, she has allowed pernicious urban forces to invade the rural, thus throwing into question the inviolability of a pastoral refuge. The dark and ancient gods of African religion have contaminated the white, middle-class home. The closing credits roll over a syncretic soundtrack that combines competing strands of choir music and drumming, sounds which suggest either the amalgam of Catholic and Yoruban forces in Santería or the conflict between Christian religion and African religion, here marked as the unresolved conflict between good and evil.

Q: The Winged Serpent

Similar themes are played out in *Q: The Winged Serpent* (1982). The feathered flying serpent is the reincarnation of the ancient god Quetzalcoatl who is prayed back into existence by an Aztec high priest who officiates over ritual human sacrifices. The objects of sacrifice are male devotees who volunteer their lives. The high priest flays the first man alive, and wears the skin like a garment. He removes the heart of the second man. These sacrifices, together with Q's practice of hunting people, serve as evidence of the inhuman cruelty and savagery of the primitive religion. Although the police eventually kill Q and destroy its nest in the Chrysler Building, the film ends with an overhead shot of an undetected egg on the rooftop of the Museum of Natural History. As in *The Believers*, the danger remains unvanquished at the end.

Columbia University figures in both films as an important signifier. First, it is the mediator between impoverished black Harlem and the white, affluent upper west side. It is a liminal figure, a fortress of white authority, maintaining class- and race-differentiated boundaries. Second, the campus is the urban equivalent of the pastoral setting, a sanctuary from the corruption of the surrounding city. Yet Columbia fails to preserve its status as gatekeeper and sanctuary; it is found to be contaminated, to house the very forces that threaten civilization. In *The Believers*, Columbia anthropologists are part of the spiritualist inner sanctum who conspire to sacrifice the protagonist's son. In *Q*, an adherent of the Aztec religion who willingly sacrifices himself is a medical student at Columbia. The University has no claim to moral discourse. In proper postmodern form, the distinction between god and monster, innocence and corruption, country and city, collapses.

African and Aztec religious lore functions in these films to estrange the dangers implicit in the inner-city setting by locating it in unfamiliar forms. Moreover, by focusing on religion, they cloak the racist dynamic operating in these films. Magical religions are equated with savagery and third-world peoples. Monstrosity is constituted as a primitive racialized evil.

HEADHUNTER

A more recent instance of race horror is *Headhunter* (1990) which, like *The Believers*, opens on a rural African tribal ceremony marked by drumming and dancing. As they sacrifice a black goat, the ritual is disrupted by the arrival of an ominous force from which the group flees. The film cuts to a ritual ceremony in Miami where a priest sacrifices a chicken and calls forth a demon who decapitates him. This scene relocates the dark and primitive religion to the United States.

The white protagonists are police detectives Catherine (Cat) Hall and Pete Giuliani who are called in to investigate a murder in a Nigerian pocket of Little Havana. The paraphernalia surrounding the decapitated Nigerian is described as "some sort of religious stuff." Baffled by the foreignness of events, the detectives consult an expert informant, Sinclair, a professor of Pan-African Studies at the University of Miami. A shaman of the Ibo tribe and the author of *Life Among the Tribes*, Sinclair calls the killer a demonic "curse." The Ibo have fled to America to escape the terror of the demon-aligned militia in Nigeria, but the terror pursues them in the form of the headhunter who comes "to reclaim the souls that have escaped his reach." The vicious demon derives his power from human executions.

Sinclair, who traverses between the world of the Ibo and the world of mainstream American culture, is the only Ibo with a speaking part in the film. He is able to decipher events for the detectives, who gradually come to accept his account. Putting aside their skepticism, Cat and Pete come to believe in the creature, a belief their captain disparages as "jungle hocus-pocus" subscribed to by "jungle bunnies." The captain serves as racist foil to Pete's liberal ideas. When Pete alludes to the racial double standard and accuses the captain of neglecting the crime because the victims are black, the captain confirms his charge by saying, "They're just negroes and they're not even our negroes." They are Other and the film confirms this devaluation.

Sinclair's function as native informant is completed when he reveals to Cat and Pete that to kill the demon they must dismember him. Soon after, Sinclair is killed for this disclosure. But armed with this knowledge, Cat is able to kill the demon with an ax. Elsewhere, the demon is resurrected.

Despite the film's feeble efforts to distance itself from racism, *Headhunter* constitutes the monster as a primitive racialized evil associated with a powerful and savage religion practiced by third-world people.

WOLFEN

Race horror's confluence of signifiers is exploited and critiqued in *Wolfen* (1981), which opens with the stalking and murder of a politically ambitious tycoon, his wife, and chauffeur in Manhattan's Battery Park. The police investigation directs suspicion at Haitian voodoo, terrorism, and American Indian activism. The voodoo thesis is introduced when a "voodoo ring" is found on the severed hand of the chauffeur, a former member of the Papa Doc secret police in Haiti. Suspicion that the deaths may have been executions performed by a terrorist organization is motivated by the tycoon's history of imperialist activities. A member of the power elite, and a descendant of a fifteenth-century Dutch settler, he is implicated in overthrowing a government, mining holy ground, and otherwise being an enemy of the third world. The police also suspect an American Indian activist who claims he can shapeshift into a werewolf.

Although the police department and private security personnel favor the terrorist explanation to the end, it is an altogether different agent that is at work. The wolfen, a highly intelligent species of wolf, are responsible for the executions. The wolfen are introduced at the opening through extended point-of-view work. Subjective camera work constructs a nonhuman, heightened mode of perception through heat vision, sonic echoes, and close to the ground fleet and nimble tracking shots. Throughout the film, unclaimed point-of-view shots, in which no part of the body to whom the look is imputed is visible, signify the presence of the wolfen. In genre conventions, this look belongs by implication to the monster.

In the course of the police investigation, the detective interrogates an American Indian elder who serves as the expert informant. The elder explains that the wolfen are survivors of an almost extinct species that lives in urban slums, "the graveyard" of the human species, where they scavenge, feeding on society's "garbage"—the homeless, drug-addicted outcasts of society. He likens the wolfen to the American Indian: members of a tribal society coexisting peacefully with other nations until subjected to genocide by European colonizers. Refugees who have gone underground to avoid detection and slaughter, these creatures kill only to survive. The wolfen killed the tycoon because he was executing plans to construct luxury condominiums in the burned out tenements of the South Bronx where they live. In effect, the tycoon was executed for practicing gentrification, which displaces local inhabitants so the rich can move in.

The elder's discourse, which the film legitimates, reverses political and moral polarities: what we call civilization (urban redevelopment) is savagery (disenfranchisement), the wolfen are more like gods than monsters. In *Wolfen*, the lost domain of innocence reemerges in the city, not in the park, but in the rubble of a collapsing church in the South Bronx. Equipped with heat vision, they readily discern lies, thereby rendering duplicity impossible among their kind. Unlike human society, where moral discourse has collapsed, wolfen society is utopian, "more complete," founded on trust and communication. The film closes with a tracking shot of the unvanquished wolfen returning home. Whereas *The Possession of Joel Delaney*, *The Believers*, *Q*, and *Headhunter* articulate the collapse of innocence and moral discourse in a society teeming with corruption emanating from a primitive racialized evil, *Wolfen*'s ancient race, associated with American Indian culture, is constituted as heroic, while dominant white society, descended from European colonists, is constituted as the corrupting influence. Although sharing some of the characteristics of the other films, *Wolfen* differs by implicating white racism as the source of evil. In this, it is similar to *The People Under the Stairs*, *Night of the Living Dead*, and *Tales from the Hood*.

Tales from the Hood

The title of *Tales from the Hood* (1995) clearly evokes the moralistic horror comics of William Gaines, the 1972 anthology film, and the contemporary television series of the same name: *Tales from the Crypt*. *Tales from the Hood* blends the horrific morality tale with the black-oriented focus of *Boyz*

'N the Hood (1991). An anthology film, *Tales from the Hood* satisfies both expectations. The first tale, "Rogue Cop Revelation," implicates the Los Angeles Police Department in the urban drug epidemic affecting the black community. After drug-dealing white cops brutalize and kill a black crusader against police corruption, he returns as a zombie to avenge himself and other victims of the racist cops. This tale's critique of the L.A.P.D. is limited by its relegation of racism to rogue cops. However, much to its credit, the film is also critical of the internecine gang warfare that rages in Los Angeles.

In the final tale, "Hard Core Convert," a drug-dealing gang member is imprisoned and undergoes a program of behavior modification that likens gang violence to Klan lynchings. Gang killings in the Hood are portrayed as playing into the genocidal agenda of the hooded Klan. This segment graphically juxtaposes scenes of black men in ski masks murdering other black men, with images of black men slaughtered by white hooded lynching parties.

We get a more nuanced critique of racism in the third tale. "K.K.K. Comeuppance" opens with a televised political campaign ad in which the camera shows a married white man opening his mail to find a job rejection notice as the voice-over intones:

> You can give it any name you want. The fact is affirmative action, quotas, reparations, all mean one thing: another qualified individual won't get a job or an education simply because he's *not* the right color. I thought that's what we were trying to get away from. Duke Medger for governor, an original American. Isn't it about time? (my transcription)

Duke Medger, gubernatorial candidate and former Klan member is an amalgam of David Duke, a former Nazi and Klansman who ran for governor of Louisiana in 1990, and Jesse Helms (Republican, North Carolina) whose 1990 Senate reelection campaign featured a similar commercial in which the announcer comments: "You needed that job, and you were the best qualified. But they had to give it to a racial minority.

Is that really fair?" (quoted in Diamond and Bates, 329). Duke Medger's private conversations are peppered with overtly racist speech, but his political campaign image resorts to such covert expressions of racism as opposition to affirmative action and attacks on welfare.

Duke lives on a former plantation whose Civil War–era owner massacred his slaves rather than allow them to be free. Legend has it that their souls were finally laid to rest when an "old voodoo woman" bought the place and transferred their souls into dolls. The promised comeuppance of the segment title is delivered by the dolls who first kill Duke's image adviser, a black man who shares Duke's vitriolic racist views, then after a protracted struggle, the dolls surround Duke and issue their own stinging bites.

Tales from the Hood deviates from race horror in significant ways. The monster is either racialized as white and associated with racism, or is a black accomplice of white racism. Only Duke Medgers is associated with religion, the Christian far right, a religion not hegemonically coded as dark and primitive. In contrast, the figures that race horror would cast as monstrous—the zombie, the voodoo woman and the dolls—are instead the heroic agents of justice. Although voodoo is presented as a powerful magical religion associated with third-world people, both the religion and its followers are coded as good. Finally, the Duke Medgers tale is not set in a city,[12] but on a former plantation to evoke the deep roots of American racism in the centuries-long practice of slavery, coded here as a form of savagery.

Although *Tales from the Hood* creates a space for antiracist discourse, this move is mitigated by a film tradition of monstrifying voodoo in films from *White Zombie* (1932) to the more recent *Angel Heart* (1987). Similarly, *Candyman* treads a thin line between critiquing and reinforcing racism.

CANDYMAN

The monster of *Candyman* (1992) is the product of white racism. The son of a freed slave, an inventor who amassed a fortune and provided him with an education, he crosses the color line when he takes a wealthy white woman as his lover and impregnates her. In retaliation, her father and a white mob turn on him. They saw off his right hand with a rusty blade, strip him, and smear his prone body with honey to draw the bees that sting him to death. Then, in proper fashion for a lynching, they burn his body. Legend has it that this act of race hatred took place on the site of the Cabrini-Green Housing Projects in Chicago.

Helen Lyle, a doctoral candidate studying urban legend at the University of Illinois becomes fascinated by reports that "Candyman" haunts Cabrini-Green. Armed with a hook, he is said to eviscerate his victims from "groin to gullet." The devastating poverty of the projects and the hostility with which white interlopers like Helen are greeted suggest that the racial injustice incarnated by Candyman persists.[13]

Rational academic that she is, Helen flouts the legend of Candyman. To repudiate superstition, she repeats his name in the mirror five times, and unwittingly summons him. She and her research partner, Bernadette Walsh, go to the projects to investigate accounts of his murders. Before long, Helen discovers Candyman's lair in an abandoned area of the projects. She steps through an entrance that looks from the outside like a ragged hole in the wall, but that from the inside can be seen to be painted to look like a gaping mouth. Although at this point, Helen still clings to her rational skepticism, the descent into Candyman's world on which she embarks will prove to be an irrevocable one.

Helen's skepticism appears to be borne out when she discovers that a gang leader uses the Candyman legend to intimidate people. Helen's willingness to prosecute him for assault destabilizes the project residents' belief in the legend. Although Helen may not believe in him, Candyman believes in her.

Unlike his other victims, like Bernadette, a black woman whom he dispatches with brutal haste, Helen becomes the object of Candyman's seduction. He leads her to a mural of the scene of his abjection, which depicts the white woman he desired. It looks like a likeness of Helen. Desiring Helen, he

FIGURE 5.2. Helen discovers Candyman's lair in the Cabrini-Green Housing Projects, *Candyman* (1992). Courtesy of Museum of Modern Art Film Still Archive.

invites her to "be my victim." But as the interracial romance of the past once conjured up disgust and loathing in the white mob, so the suggestion of intimate contact with Candyman conjures up body horror in the audience.[14] Aside from the conspicuous hook implanted in his stump, there is the matter of Candyman's decomposed body cavity which, as he reveals to her, is swarming with bees. When they kiss, bees stream from his mouth. Thus, body horror operates here to undermine the acceptability of interracial romance.

Although Candyman wants a willing victim, he is determined to take her, in part because her disbelief cost him his followers. He wants "believers," for without people's fear he is nothing. To possess Helen and get his congregation back, he executes an elaborate plan that results in Helen's death. In the end, Helen becomes Candyman.[15] She appears when inadvertently summoned by her unfaithful and guilt-wracked husband who repeats her name five times into the mirror, and like Candyman she kills him with a hook. This scene betrays the film's affinity with the slasher film, where the protagonist is likely to be an intrepid white woman who displays agency. But the film also falls prey to the slasher film's tendency to contain the woman's agency by making good on the threat to her life.

In the end, *Candyman* depicts both the white woman and the black man as monstrous, but this does not necessarily mean that the film lacks a critical dimension. Considering that a sexist society perceives battered women who kill in self-defense as criminal, if not monstrous, and that a racist society appraises aggressive black men (and sometimes women) as criminals, if not monsters, then is there not some pleasure and sense of power to be gained, at least by female and black audience members,[16] from seeing the power in these violent figures?[17] I believe there is, and that a film like *Candyman* lends itself well to this subversive reading strategy. But this reading strategy would be much more difficult to sustain with films, like *The Believers* or *Headhunter*, that readily embrace the construction of the primitive and savage racial Other. Nevertheless, the race horror film is in a position to perform a critique of white racism, as is the case in *Wolfen* or *Tales from the Hood*, and this is where its critical potential lies.

AFTERWORD

The contemporary horror film genre is a combination of feminist and antifeminist elements. It contains racist and antiracist impulses. It criticizes and endorses hierarchical relations of power. In short, it is a mix of contradictory tendencies. Subgenres and individual films play out these contradictory pulls in different combinations and with varying emphases. While the slasher film is at heart subversive in its depiction of female agency, the race horror film is basically conservative in its portrayal of a savage racial Other. The countervailing tendencies in films of both subgenres that belie these generalizations leave open the possibility for both antifeminist readings of the slasher film and antiracist readings of the race horror film. My point is not to fix the meanings of these films once and for all but rather to point to the critical potential within the genre that comprises a significant source of the pleasure that fans derive from viewing these films. Critics who ignore the contradictory elements of the genre do a disservice to the complex readings of which audiences are capable.

There is a parallel between the conflicting elements of the genre and the tension implicit in recreational terror. As much an exercise in mastery as in terror, the roller coaster ride of horror film viewing is one in which controlled loss substitutes for loss of control. It is a ride in which fans play at victimization and monstrosity, and enter a world where logic founders and the fragility of the human body is evidenced, all from the safety of a theater, or living room, seat. Recreational terror provides the framework that allows viewers to pleasurably submit to the tension and fear provoked by the highly conventionalized spectacle of violence that characterizes the contemporary horror film. It is in this protected context that fans derive pleasure from the genre's rehearsal of the fear of injury and death in a world where safety is, in every sense of the term, a fiction.

The genre audience acquires a taste for the destructuring tendency of the contemporary horror film, and a willingness not to resist but to relish it. *Scream* (1997), Wes Craven's latest entry into the slasher film, takes seriously the premise that teenaged audiences of the horror film draw on ample reserves of insider knowledge about the genre. The film's horror-savvy characters continuously comment not only on the horror videos they watch but also on the murders occurring in the story. In this vein, the teenagers killed at the outset of the film are described by a friend as "splatter movie-killed." In addition, *Scream* places its characters in a larger tabloid-saturated context. The grisly murders are featured on, among others, a television tabloid show called *Top Story*, a show that presents "real-life" murders as entertainment.

Horror references abound in the film. The first victim is tested on her knowledge of horror film trivia. The high school janitor, Fred, is dressed like Freddy Krueger. The protagonist, Sidney, is teased that she is "starting to sound like some Wes Carpenter flick." Characters in the film watch *Halloween* on video. Randy, the nerdy character who works in a video store, insists that the police are ineffectual because they do not watch horror movies. If they did, they would realize that "everybody's a suspect." Randy, an exemplary competent audience member, summarizes the "rules" of how to survive a horror movie. First, he says, you must be a virgin. Second, you must never say "I'll be right back," or venture out alone to investigate a noise.

The characters' running commentary on the slasher film demonstrates not only the acuity of horror fans but also the degree to which the conventions of the subgenre have become domesticated through repetition. *Scream* strives to overcome this routinization by transgressing some conventions. The killer turns out to be two males working in tandem. The nerd, usually a victim, survives. Two females—Sidney and Gale Weathers, the tabloid reporter, neither of whom are virgins—not only survive but join forces to do so. Finally, the film offers a female-friendly closed ending in which the killers are left unambiguously dead. The conclusion of *Scream* capitalizes, both critically and commercially, on the feminist potential of the slasher film, the preeminent Hollywood genre that shows women using self-defense effectively despite harrowing circumstances.

For the fan viewer, the horror film provides an exquisite exercise in coping with the terrors of everyday life. For the cultural analyst, the critical potential of the feminist and antiracist tendencies of contemporary cinematic horror cannot be overlooked. Delving through the dense thicket of intertwining and contradictory impulses that comprise the genre may be a hazardous journey, but it is well worth taking.

NOTES

INTRODUCTION

1. The uneasy relationship between postmodernism and feminism can be illustrated in the debate over the category of "women." For theorists such as Jean-François Lyotard, postmodernism rejects universalizing categories like "women" as ahistorical and essentialist. But to repudiate all generalizations about structural inequality is to nullify the project of feminism that is grounded in the ability to make general political claims about "women" as a systematically oppressed category. One way out of this dilemma, as Nancy Fraser and Linda Nicholson (1990) suggest, is to make critical social theory historical and contingent.

CHAPTER ONE. RECREATIONAL TERROR AND THE POSTMODERN ELEMENTS OF THE CONTEMPORARY HORROR FILM

1. By films that cultural consensus defines as horror I mean those that are treated as horror by televisual and print reviewers like Siskel and Ebert, academic critics like Linda Williams, commentaries like Kim Newman's *Nightmare Movies*, coffee table books like John McCarty's *Splatter Movies*, the classification schemes of video rental stores, and the film industry's classification through advertisements. It is by these terms that the films I have selected for study are regularly, though not necessarily unanimously, discussed as horror films.

2. Social theorists disagree on how (or even whether) to periodize postmodernism. For instance, Hal Foster locates the post-

modern break in the late fifties to early sixties (1983, xiii), whereas Todd Gitlin does so "after the sixties" (1989, 353).

3. For an opposing account, see Rhona Berenstein (1990) who argues that the classical horror film draws a more ambiguous and unstable universe than is commonly believed.

4. In the late fifties gothic monsters reemerged primarily in English films such as *The Curse of Frankenstein* (1957), *Dracula* (1958), and *The Curse of the Werewolf* (1960). These English gothics constitute a transitional form of the genre. From the classical paradigm they draw the familiar retinue of monsters, the use of exotic time/place and male experts. From the postmodern paradigm they draw an ambiguous boundary between good and evil, and the use of graphic, sexualized violence. See Pirie (1974) and Hutchings (1993) for excellent treatments of this tradition.

5. Brophy (1986) periodizes the genre somewhat differently than I do; he locates the contemporary genre as a "post-1975" phenomenon, though he includes *Night of the Living Dead* (1968) and *The Exorcist* (1973) in his discussion.

6. *Dr. Jekyll and Sister Hyde* transgresses the boundary between male and female in provocative ways. Dr. Jekyll butchers women to extract the ovaries he needs for his feminizing metamorphosis, and in the process becomes Jack the Ripper. As the experiment progresses, his feminine alter ego becomes the dominant figure who continues to commit Jack the Ripper murders despite his resistance. Adding a new wrinkle to the history of male violence, the film transforms this mythic figure of male misogyny into a female figure.

7. See Creed (1993) for a fuller development of how Kristeva's work on abjection applies to the horror film.

8. I gratefully acknowledge Michael Brown's use of this metaphor in a personal communication, circa 1990.

9. Christopher Sharrett (1984) observes, although try as I might I do not, that the temporal order collapses in the final sequence of *The Texas Chain Saw Massacre.* Describing the dinner table scene at which Sally is seated, bound, sometimes gagged, and always tormented by the cannibalistic trio of killers, Sharrett notes that, "It is night when the party begins, dawn when Sally crashes through a window and escapes, and late afternoon as she is pursued down the road by Leatherface and his brother" (269).

10. Like *Targets* (also 1968), *Night of the Living Dead*, in an acutely self-reflexive moment, uses Boris Karloff as a signifier of the anachronistic monster. In the cemetery, when Johnny notices that Barbra is frightened, he taunts her in an imitation of Karloff's signature voice. "They're coming to get you Baarrbra." The zombie who then attacks her is a Karloff look-alike. For an excellent discussion of *Night of the Living Dead*, see Dillard (1987).

11. To some extent sequels temper this thrust toward closure in the classical paradigm. This is especially evident in *The Bride of Frankenstein* (1935), which picks up near the end of *Frankenstein* and rewrites it so that the creature escapes.

12. Ironically, the kinder, gentler days of horror are historically characterized by virulent racism. Police arrest the school's black janitor who is, as one cop acknowledges, a scapegoat people are more than ready to condemn during this period of struggle over school desegregation (1962).

13. See Williams (1977, 121–27) for a discussion of "Dominant, Residual, and Emergent" cultural elements as they relate to historical change.

14. A notable variation of this paradigm is the infrequent ending form in which the monster, defeated or not, is revealed to be a symptom of the normative order that is corrupt. Society itself is implicated in the outbreak of evil. An early instance of this is *Peeping Tom* (1960). Later instances include science-fiction oriented nature-gone-awry films, such as *Prophecy* (1979) and *Alligator* (1980).

15. Similar to *Invaders from Mars*, *Not of this Earth* (1957) ends not with the dominant but with the emergent feature, i.e., not with the defeat of the alien but with the appearance of another (as yet unsuspected) alien.

16. Both versions of *The Thing* are based on John Campbell Jr.'s novella "Who Goes There?" (1938). Although the 1982 film draws more narrative detail from the novella than the 1951 version, the tenor of the close-ended story lives more in the 1951 film. In the novella, community solidarity abounds and human agency prevails.

17. Tudor speaks of how effectively vampires and psychotics pass as ordinary people in the everyday world of paranoid horror (1989, 104).

18. Jean Baudrillard (1983) identifies the postmodern with the triumph of the simulacra, copies without originals. For Baudrillard, in the postmodern, the distinction between original and copy is destroyed, and simulation is experienced as more real than the real.

19. There are historical and narrative links between horror and nightmares. Key horror stories inspired by nightmares include Mary Shelley's *Frankenstein* (1818), Bram Stoker's *Dracula* (1897), and Robert Louis Stevenson's *Dr. Jekyll and Mr. Hyde* (1886). Nightmares have been featured in a myriad of horror films: *Dead of Night, Invaders from Mars*, and *A Nightmare on Elm Street* (series) to name a few.

20. For a discussion of gimmickry, see Castle (1976) and, Vale and Juno (1986).

21. The original *Halloween* introduces Michael Meyers, but Jason Voorhees does not appear as the killer until *Friday the 13th: Part 2* (1981). In the original *A Nightmare on Elm Street* the killer is called Fred Krueger or Krueger. It is not until *A Nightmare on Elm Street Part 2: Freddy's Revenge* (1985) that he acquires the familiar "Freddy" and a less sinister appearance.

22. Other characters also play themselves in the acutely self-reflexive *New Nightmare* including John Saxon (Nancy's father), Robert Englund (Freddy Krueger), and Robert Shaye (producer of the series). Fittingly, in the credits Freddy Krueger is listed as playing himself. Further, the closing credits include a cryptic statement that "some parts of this motion picture were inspired by actual events." Publicity material in *Fangoria* (Oct. 1994), a horror film fan magazine, explains that Craven's script for *New Nightmare* drew on the experience of actress Heather Langenkamp who was stalked by a fan in the wake of her work on television (see Shapiro 43–44).

23. Examples of serializations in the thirties and forties include: *Frankenstein* (1931), *Bride of Frankenstein* (1935), *Son of Frankenstein* (1939), *Ghost of Frankenstein* (1942), *Frankenstein Meets the Wolf Man* (1943), *House of Frankenstein* (1944), *Abbott and Costello Meet Frankenstein* (1948); *The Mummy* (1932), *Mummy's Boys* (1936), *The Mummy's Hand* (1940), *The Mummy's Tomb* (1942), *The Mummy's Ghost* (1944), *The Mummy's Curse* (1944); *Dracula* (1931), *Mark of the Vampire* (1935), *Dracula's Daughter* (1936), *Son of Dracula* (1943), *Return of the Vampire* (1944).

24. Vera Dika (1990, 21) treats the appropriative strategies of pastiche in the "stalker" cycle as a mark of postmodernism.

25. The play with intertextuality presupposes not only an audience with a history of film viewing but also an audience with a history of literary horror consumption. In *Day of the Dead*, a domesticated zombie reads *Pet Sematary*, a Stephen King novel about zombies. Is this is a wry comment on the mental acuity of the horror fan, the self-reflexivity of the genre, or both?

26. Critics of horror generally regard the turn toward cannibalization and camp humor as portending its deterioration. See, for instance, Hardy (1986, 46) and Newman (1988, 211). Similarly, Rick Altman (1987, 117–21) sees the self-reflexive turn as an almost inevitable stage for all genres, a point at which the genre confronts its own shortcomings.

27. Similarly, William Paul in a lengthy study of "gross-out" in horror and comedy called *Laughing Screaming* emphasizes the ambivalent character of gross-out. "As it is a mode moving in two directions at once, the horror films may invoke comedy, while the comedies may take on suddenly nightmarish imagery" (1994, 419).

Chapter Two. The Pleasure of Seeing/Not-Seeing the Spectacle of the Wet Death

1. For further discussion of this camera work, see Carroll on "unassigned camera movement" (1990, 155), Giles on "motivated camera movement" (1984, 44), Dika on the "moving camera POV shot" (1987, 88), and Clover on the "I-camera" (1987, 190).

2. J. P. Telotte (1990) is speaking of the broader rubric of fantasy films.

3. Barbara Creed's designation of not-looking as the fifth look of cinema adds to the four looks characterized by others: (1) the look of the camera (2) the look of a fictional character within narrative space (3) the look of the spectator at the screen, and (4) the direct look at the camera by a narrative character.

4. The dialectic in recreational terror between seeing and not-seeing is reminiscent of Freud's fort-da game, in which a child rehearses the loss and return of his mother, in an attempt to master

his fear of separation. Similarly, recreational terror rehearses the loss of control through a controlled loss. See Freud, *Beyond the Pleasure Principle*, for a discussion of the fort-da game and the compulsion to repeat as a way to master trauma.

5. See Dadoun, "Fetishism in the Horror Film," and Neale, *Genre* for Freudian readings of the divided attitude.

6. See Sanjek for a discussion of the horror fanzine.

7. Although Daniel Dervin (1990) is referring to fan magazines that profile actors' lives, the impulse he describes is applicable to the special-effects magazine.

8. Brophy attributes the "You've got to be fucking kidding!" wallop to the "mind-boggling" state-of-the-art special-effects makeup used in *The Thing* (1982).

9. The connection between pornography and horror is expressed in the fascination with pornography which some horror films evince. For instance *The Howling*, a film concerned with the expression and suppression of bodily appetites, opens with the protagonist, a television anchorwoman, meeting a serial killer in a pornographic den. The killer traps her in a screening room and proceeds to change into a werewolf to the strobe effect of the hard-core film.

10. Richard Gehr uses the term "carnography" in a review of splatterpunk novels. The comparison I make between gore and porn is indebted to Linda Williams's (1989) work on mainstream heterosexual pornography.

11. Andrew Tudor issues this disclaimer in the context of describing a 1972 horror film that features sexual activity. Linda Williams, to her credit, acknowledges her defensiveness and points out that if she admits to pleasure in pornography, she stands to be discredited not simply for enjoying sexual materials but because she is a *woman* enjoying sexual materials. As a male scholar, Noel Carroll is free to exclaim that he had "a hell of a good time" writing his book on the horror film (1990, 11). In contrast, opponents of these genres deny the horror or porn film's ability to entice them into pleasure but freely express their arousal as righteous condemnation.

12. During a classroom screening of *The Texas Chain Saw Massacre*, a colleague passing in the hall looked in to see what film we were watching. Hearing the woman's groans and lack of dialogue, he

mistook it for a pornographic film. What he overlooked in his initial assessment was the absence of the insipid musical soundtrack that anchors hard-core sex scenes.

13. Although Williams (1989a, 191) classifies *Snuff* as "a variant of the slasher film," one that despite its special-effects violence tries to pass itself off as a snuff film, the category of snuff, characterized by actual deadly violence, is distinct from the slasher or horror film.

14. A related but distinct genre is the "mondo" film. Like the early cinema's exotic travelogues, the mondo film depicts bizarre behavior, including genuine violence, from around the world. The first such film was *Mondo Cane* (1963), released the same year as the first gore film, *Blood Feast*. The mondo genre peaked in the sixties, disappeared, then reemerged with *Faces of Death* (1978), a pseudo-documentary video (series) which purports to compile unstaged scenes of real-life death and violence (Vale and Juno 1986, 153–56).

15. Wes Craven interview on the television program "Anatomy of Horror" which aired on August 22, 1995, on WWOR (NYC).

16. Stephen King (1981, 60–61) also asserts the preeminence of these three figures, and treats their respective novels as horror literature's canonical works.

Chapter Three. . . . And Then She Killed Him: Women and Violence in the Slasher Film

1. Unless otherwise indicated, I will be citing from Dika's article, "The Stalker Film: 1978–81." Dika's book, *Games of Terror*, bears the same predictable character as the slasher films she describes: the book, as the sequel to the article, simply remakes what it copies and does so less effectively.

2. Unless otherwise indicated, all Clover references will be to *Men, Women and Chain Saws*, and all Creed references will be to *The Monstrous-Feminine*.

3. Dika's sole acknowledgment of the issue of female spectatorship comes when she rejects the psychoanalytic reading (à la Mulvey) that she herself puts forth as one which disregards female psychology. Her purpose is not to provide a different account of female psychology but to advance the argument that the surviving

female of the slasher film represents an enfeebled but rallying America in the period of transition from the Carter to the Reagan administrations (1987, 97–99). In *Games of Terror*, she abandons any notion of the female spectator and treats the viewer as male.

4. Clover (1987, 224; 1992, 6–7) cites Twitchell (1985, 68–72) to support her claim that the primary horror film audience is not only adolescent but male. However, Twitchell, on the basis of "personal observations," attests only to the adolescent character of this audience. Although he notes the presence of "rogue males" who are older and watch alone, he also points to the larger presence of females who watch in groups, couples, or non-dating pairs. Caputi (1990, 9) cites Clover (1987, 224) to assert that "all observers agree" on the adolescent male character of the horror film audience.

5. According to Mulvey (1985, 311) the woman's body evokes not only pleasure but castration anxiety in the male spectator, a danger negotiated through two cinematic solutions. One is to fetishize the female body, to disavow her castration by substituting a part of her body for the absent phallus. The second is to reenact her castration. In this voyeuristic operation, the woman is investigated, found wanting, and her sexual guilt established as the grounds for her punishment.

6. The subtitle for this section was inspired by Lynda Hart's dedication in *Fatal Women* (1994, v): "For Aileen Wuornos and for all the women who have been vilified, pathologized, and murdered for defending themselves by whatever means necessary."

7. Negotiation is generally useless. But in *Friday the 13th, Part 2* (1981), the surviving female (Alice) impersonates Jason's dead mother and effectively commands him to put down his weapon.

8. If we consider that vigilance and a healthy dose of suspicion are the keystones of self-defense, we can further see how the surviving female's paranoia operates as a "productive fear." Judith Halberstam, who unlike most critics of the horror film recognizes that horror can be empowering to female viewers, writes: "Films that feature sadistic murderers stalking unsuspecting female victims simply confirm a certain justified paranoia which means that women aren't crazy to be paranoid about rape and murder but rather they are crazy not to be" (1995, 165).

9. Through most of the 1968 *Night of the Living Dead*, Barbra is passive, but in the 1990 version she is remade into Barbara, a char-

acter who fights boldly, starting with the initial attack in the cemetery. Through the course of the film, she sheds her impractical pumps and skirt for the hardier boots and pants she finds in the farmhouse. Furthermore, it is Barbara who first notices the zombies converging on the house and who initiates the defensive boarding of the windows. Finally, it is she who realizes that the zombies are so slow that, armed with a gun for back up, she could elude them on foot. In the end, that is how she survives.

10. Masculine and feminine are more than human characteristics; they are basic metaphysical categories that organize the cultural field. Power is coded masculine even when embodied in a biological female. Consider the following joke:

> Q: "Why doesn't Margaret Thatcher wear pants?"
> A: "Because her balls might show."

The female status of the former Prime Minister of England, also known as the Iron Lady, is neutralized through a masculinization that distorts reality to conform to social restrictions on accession to (male) power.

11. Although I do not agree with Clover's psychoanalytic reduction of the surviving female to a male in drag, her reading, together with Creed's, does suggest that male viewers incorporate the power of the surviving female as their own to compensate for the threat of female power.

12. In "Visual Pleasure and Narrative Cinema," Mulvey posits a sexual division of labor in the process of film viewing. The male viewer is positioned as the subject of the gaze, i.e., to identify voyeuristically with the look of the camera or narcissistically with the male protagonist. In contrast, the female viewer is positioned as the object of the gaze, i.e., to identify narcissistically with the female body imbued with "to-be-looked-at-ness" (309). In "Afterthoughts," a subsequent reworking of these ideas, Mulvey argues that the female spectator can partially appropriate the male gaze, can identify with narrative agency and active desire, but she is masculinized in the process. So thoroughly are positions of narrative agency and active desire coded as masculine and relegated to male characters in Mulvey's analysis, that the female gaze is at best a fe*male* gaze, a transvestite experience. Fortunately, this limited construction of the female gaze has been challenged by critics (Gamman 1989, 2–5; Stacey 1994, 19–26) who argue for a more contradictory

reading of popular culture, one less wedded to the psychoanalytic approach favored by Mulvey, a perspective that informs my work.

13. For an intriguing discussion of the typical homicide as an experience of "righteously enraged slaughter," see Jack Katz, *Seductions of Crime.*

14. This chapter draws on Lentz's (1993) excellent discussion of women-and-gun films, which in many ways parallel the slasher film in at least some of the films she discusses (*Blue Steel, Thelma and Louise, The Silence of the Lambs*).

15. This observation is based on informal conversations with friends and acquaintances who responded to my research topic with fascination about why I would subject myself to such torture.

16. Heather Levi, personal communication, circa 1990. Also, the story of female rage is the flip side of the rape story. The story of Lorena Bobbitt's mutilating act of retribution against her husband John Bobbitt provokes different reactions in men than in women. As the castrating woman she horrifies men but she represents something different to women. Part of her appeal for women is the poetic justice of the pound of flesh she exacted from the man who raped her. What provides the moral alibi for enjoying this guilty or not-so-guilty pleasure is its extreme rarity. Nationally, men routinely rape women; women seldom castrate men. For a detailed discussion of rape-revenge films see Clover 1992.

17. The resourcefulness of the postmodern horror genre is demonstrated in the "final" entry in the *Nightmare on Elm Street* series, *New Nightmare* in which Nancy is brought back through an ingenious plot twist. Heather Langenkamp plays "herself," in effect reprising her role as Nancy. In this film, Freddie exceeds his cinematic reach when he kills people "in real life" associated with the series' production. Heather/Nancy must and does kill him.

18. Mary Beth Haralovich points out that the suburban family sit-coms that proliferated in the late fifties and early sixties drew nostalgically on earlier historical conditions (1992, 112). See Haralovich for an interesting discussion of the ideological function of these shows. I am indebted to Anne Rubenstein for her help in clarifying my understanding of the relationship between the Republican ideology of family values and the historical period to which it alludes (pers. com. 8/96).

19. David Edelstein presciently provides a powerful reason for the success of *The Stepfather* on video when he suggests that putting Jerry Blake on the television screen side by side with other television dads like Jim Anderson and Ward Cleaver is going to make the film "blaze up like a dream" (1987, 54).

20. Two sequels, *Stepfather 2: Make Room for Daddy* (1989) and *Stepfather 3* (1992) do not pose a threat to this film's surviving females. The sequels are essentially dim remakes that substitute a young boy for the teenage girl and bring back the killer but continue no other original character.

Chapter Four. The Cultural Politics of the Postmodern Horror Film

1. As Jeffrey Pence points out in "Terror Incognito" a number of Henry's victims are played by the same actress (1994, 532). According to the credits listed in *Sight and Sound*, Mary Demas plays two of the victims in the opening montage of death: the first victim shown lying in the grassy field and the prostitute in the bathroom. Demas also plays one of the two hookers Henry and Otis pick up and then kill (Newman 1991, 43). It's always the same and it's always different, indeed.

2. Murders committed in *Henry: Portrait of a Serial Killer*

	Off-screen	*On-screen*	*Total*
Females	7 female	3 female	10
Males	2 male	4 male	6
Total	9	7	16

3. The centrality of the snuff videotape in the film prompted some critics to report that *Henry* was financed by MPI, the company which distributes the *Faces of Death* video series. See for example Carr (1990, 69) and Sherman (1990, 8).

4. There is almost no academic discussion of the element of sexual stimulation in recreational terror. Although Creed (1993, 3) wonders if male viewers experience erections to compensate for the castration anxiety triggered by watching horror films, she fails to consider the possibility of female sexual arousal. Robin Wood touches on the subject of sexual arousal in his discussion of *Last House on the Left* (1972). He suggests that the scene in which Phyl-

lis is killed and disemboweled is the most disturbing moment in the film. The director, Wes Craven, describes this scene, which appears to have been cut from existing prints.

> The killing of Phyllis is very sexual in feeling, and ended with her being stabbed not only by the men but by the woman repeatedly. Then she fell to the ground and Sadie bent down and pulled out a loop of her intestines. They looked at it and that's where it all stopped. That's when they realized what they had done, and they looked at each other and walked away. They were disgusted at what they had done (quoted in Wood 1986, 127–28).

What is so disturbing about this scene is the simultaneous humanity and inhumanity of the violators. What is so disturbing about this film is that it evokes feelings the audience did not know were there (125).

5. Anonymous, personal communication, August 1995.

6. Anonymous, personal communication, May 1995.

7. Although I disagree with Jane Caputi's (1990) argument that the celebrity of screen monsters such as Freddy and Jason legitimate male violence against women in everyday life, she does make the valuable point that to define serial killers as enigmas is to ignore the patently misogynous character of the dominant culture (6).

8. Historically, the recognition of and fascination with serial killers emerged in the late sixties when highly visible forms of violence like the Vietnam War, race riots, political assassinations, and police brutality activated a marked increase in the concern with violence and in screen depictions of violence. The serial killer came to personify the widespread violence of American society. Moreover, to understand the significance of the serial killer we must situate him as a product of late capitalist society, one who stands in opposition to the culture of money. Impervious to money, it is not possible to buy your way out of a serial killer's clutches. In a culture that understands value primarily in terms of money, this truly is an enigma. The proliferation of books and movies analyzing or depicting serial killers (together with the market in such collectibles as T-shirts, comic books, and trading cards) is at least in part an attempt to domesticate this anticapitalist impulse by commodifying them.

CHAPTER FIVE.
RACE HORROR

1. Noel Carroll (1984) examines the racial subtext of *King Kong* (1933) in which a racial Other from an exotic location populated by Black "natives" is enslaved and brought by ship to New York City, where he is displayed in shackles for the profit of his captors. Lester Friedman (1984) explores films that figure the Jew as monster. Judith Halberstam (1995, esp. 77–84) analyzes the racial discourse of literary and filmic versions of *Dr. Jekyll and Mr. Hyde*, texts that figure Hyde as a monster whose body combines "Semitic and Negroid features" (82). Rhona Berenstein (1996) investigates the fear of miscegenation expressed in "jungle-horror" films including *King Kong* (160–97).

2. For a Foucauldian analysis of the primacy of the gendered Other in horror, see Judith Halberstam's excellent book, *Skin Shows: Gothic Horror and the Technology of Monsters* (1995).

3. For a fascinating account of the redneck in city-revenge films, see Clover, esp. 114–37, 154–65.

4. See Raymond Williams's *The Country and the City* (1973) for a Marxist analysis of the English literary uses of country and city as contrasting structures of feeling. The country is associated with the pastoral, the realm of innocence, whereas the city is associated with disturbance and corruption.

5. This slasher film, *Friday the 13th Part 8: Jason Takes Manhattan*, cleverly exploited the iconoclastic urban twist in its title and ad campaign. The television ad featured Jason, the killer, standing on the Brooklyn Heights Promenade overlooking the Manhattan skyline to the tune of Frank Sinatra's "New York, New York." Similarly, the subway poster campaign in New York condensed two icons—Jason's signature hockey mask and the "I Love New York" motto—by inscribing a hockey mask in place of the *o* in the word *love*. But despite this persistent invocation of the city, only two short scenes take place in Times Square. The scenes supposedly set on Manhattan's waterfront and subway system look nothing like Manhattan. Indeed, the film alludes to its Vancouver shooting location when Jason gazes quizzically at a billboard ad for a hockey league.

6. A wave of black urban uprisings began with Watts in 1965, and peaked between 1967 and 1968, the year *Night of the Living Dead* was released.

7. See Michael Rogin's excellent discussion of racial politics in "'The Sword Became a Flashing Vision: D.W. Griffith's *The Birth of a Nation*." The racist legacy of *Birth* can also be seen in *March of the Wooden Soldiers* (1934), a fairy tale operetta in which the evil Barnaby leads a "boogeymen" army to invade Toyland so he can abduct and "marry" the blonde and virginal Bo Peep. Toyland is rescued by the wooden soldiers who drive out the monstrous creatures and restore order. There are disturbing parallels between this sequence in *March* and the abduction in *Birth* of the blonde and virginal Elsie by Silas Lynch, the mulatto who wants to "marry" her. Lynch holds power with the help of a black army that overruns the town, until the Klan rides to the rescue. Although both films draw on the conventions of the melodrama, they also draw on the mythic figure of the black brute rapist.

8. The 1990 remake of *Night of the Living Dead* similarly casts all the living dead as white and features a black male character named Ben. But the central tension of this film revolves around gender rather than race conflict. Although still a resourceful and sympathetic character, Ben's power struggle with Harry is characterized as counterproductive squabbling by Barbara, who in this version is the empowered female whose discernment of the situation helps her survive.

9. Since economic exploitation is coded as neither violent nor monstrous in a capitalist society, *The People Under the Stairs* establishes the landlords' monstrous violence in their mutilation and abuse of young captives.

10. *Scream, Blacula, Scream,* although at heart a blaxploitation film, also treats voodoo as a magical religion whose power can be put to good or evil use. Blacula is resurrected by the performance of voodoo ritual. Convinced of voodoo's power, Blacula seeks out a powerful practitioner named Lisa Fortier. He asks her to exorcise him of his demon so he can find peace. She agrees but the ceremony is interrupted by the police. When Lisa sees Blacula kill the cops who stand in his way, she is horrified and stops him by stabbing his voodoo doll likeness through the heart.

11. Taussig (1987) is referring specifically to Indians in Colombia.

12. Although "K.K.K. Comeuppance" is not set in a city, *Tales from the Hood* as a whole alludes to Los Angeles through its title

and the focus on Black gang culture in both the framing narrative and the last tale of the film.

13. Shortly before *Candyman* was released, on October of 1992, a seven-year-old was killed by sniper fire as he walked through Cabrini-Green on his way to school. According to a *New York Times* article, the news coverage that resulted turned Cabrini-Green into a "national symbol of the ravages of poverty, gang violence and government neglect" (Terry A10). No mention is made in the article, published in early November, of the box-office success of *Candyman*, which may have contributed to the notoriety.

14. See Halberstam (1995, 5) for a similar reading of *Candyman*.

15. The sequel, *Candyman: Farewell to the Flesh* (1995), does not feature Helen; it merely remakes *Candyman* with the female lead played by Candyman's descendant, a product of the miscegenation punished in the legend.

16. Although most critics of the horror film treat the horror audience as white and middle class, in my experience the audience is both class- and race-diversified. See Dika (1990, 9) for a similar observation. Writing of the audience for *The Exorcist*, William Paul claims that it was made up of "large numbers of teenagers and lower-class blacks" (1994, 289). He also quotes Stephen Farber who characterizes the audience for this film as being "at least one-third black" (480). Perhaps *The Exorcist* is unrepresentative of horror film attendance, or perhaps class and racial diversity holds for urban but not suburban audiences, or perhaps African Americans attend horror films in the same numbers that they attend other genres, especially teenage-oriented ones. According to Guerrero (1993, 165) blacks make up about 25 to 30 percent of the box-office audience. This would make black people a sizable portion of the horror film audience.

17. Similarly, Nick De Genova (1995) argues that the violent imagery and posturing of gangster rap can be a resource for the production of black male agency. I am grateful to Heather Levi for drawing my attention to this point (pers. com. 11/96).

BIBLIOGRAPHY

Altman, Rick. *The American Film Musical.* Bloomington: Indiana UP, 1987.

Arnold, Gary. "'Henry' Hits with Reality of Random Violent Acts." *Washington Times.* 4 May 1990: E1.

Bart, Pauline, and Patricia O'Brien. "Stopping Rape: Effective Avoidance Strategies." *Signs* 10.1 (1984): 83–101.

Baudrillard, Jean. *Simulations.* New York: Semiotext(e), 1983.

Benson, Sheila. "The Heart of Darkeness in 'Portrait of a Serial Killer.'" *Los Angeles Times.* 18 Apr. 1990: F1.

Berenstein, Rhona. *Attack of the Leading Ladies: Gender, Sexuality, and Spectatorship.* New York: Columbia UP, 1996.

Bordwell, David, and Kristin Thompson. *Film Art: An Introduction.* New York: Alfred Knopf, 1979.

Boss, Pete. "Vile Bodies and Bad Medicine." *Screen* 27 (Jan/Feb 1986): 14–24.

Boston Women's Health Book Collective. *The New Our Bodies, Ourselves.* New York: Simon and Schuster, 1984 (orig. 1976).

Brophy, Philip. "Horrality: The Textuality of Contemporary Horror Films." *Screen* 27 (Jan/Feb 1986): 2–13.

Butler, Judith. "Gender Trouble, Feminist Theory, and Psychoanalytic Discourse." In *Feminism/Postmodernism.* Ed. Linda Nicholson. New York: Routledge, 1990. 324–40.

Campbell, John Jr. "Who Goes There?" [1938] repr. in *The Science Fiction Hall of Fame, Vol. IIA*. Ed. Ben Bova. New York: Avon 1974. 48–104.

Caputi, Jane. "The New Founding Fathers: The Love and Lure of the Serial Killer in Contemporary Culture." *Journal of American Culture* 13.3 (Fall 1990): 1–12.

Carr, Jay. "The Stark Horror of a Serial Killer." *Boston Globe*. 5 Jan. 1990: 69.

Carroll, Noel. "*King Kong*: Ape and Essence." In *Planks of Reason: Essays on the Horror Film*. Ed. Barry Keith Grant. Metuchen, NJ: Scarecrow Press, 1984. 215–44.

———. *The Philosophy of Horror: or Paradoxes of the Heart*. New York: Routledge, 1990.

Castle, William. *Step Right Up! I'm Gonna Scare the Pants Off America*. New York: Pharos Books, 1976.

Clover, Carol. "Her Body, Himself: Gender in the Slasher Film." *Representations* 20 (Fall 1987): 187–228.

———. *Men, Women and Chain Saws: Gender in the Modern Horror Film*. Princeton: Princeton UP, 1992.

Cohen, Ralph. "Do Postmodern Genres Exist?" In *Postmodern Genres*. Ed. Marjorie Perloff. Norman: U of Oklahoma P, 1988. 11–27.

Cowie, Elizabeth. "Fantasia." *m/f* 1 (1984): 71–104.

Creed, Barbara. *The Monstrous-Feminine: Film, Feminism, Psychoanalysis*. New York: Routledge, 1993.

Dadoun, Roger. "Fetishism in the Horror Film." [1970] repr. in *Enclitic* 1.2 (1979): 39–63.

Davies, Lyell. "*The Texas Chain Saw Massacre* and the Endtime." Paper submitted, Hunter College, Nov. 1996.

De Genova, Nick. "Gangster Rap and Nihilism in Black America: Some Questions of Life and Death." *Social Text* 43 (Fall 1995): 89–132.

De Lauretis, Teresa. *Alice Doesn't: Feminism, Semiotics, Cinema*. Bloomington: Indiana UP, 1984.

Dervin, Daniel. "Primal Conditions and Conventions: The Genre of Science Fiction." [1980] repr. in *Alien Zone: Cultural Theory and Contemporary Science Fiction Cinema*. Ed. Annette Kuhn. London: Verso, 1990. 96–102.

Diamond, Edwin, and Stephen Bates. *The Spot: The Rise of Political Advertising on Television*. Cambridge, MA: MIT P, 1992.

Dika, Vera. "The Stalker Film, 1978–81." In *American Horrors: Essays on the Modern American Horror Film*. Ed. Gregory Waller. Chicago: U of Illinois P, 1987. 86–101.

———. *Games of Terror: Halloween, Friday the 13th, and the Films of the Stalker Genre*. Rutherford, NJ: Fairleigh Dickinson UP, 1990.

Dillard, R.H.W. "*Night of the Living Dead*: It's Not Just a Wind That's Passing Through." In *American Horrors: Essays on the Modern American Horror Film*. Ed. Gregory Waller. Chicago: U of Illinois P, 1987. 14–29.

Di Stefano, Christine. "Dilemmas of Difference: Feminism, Modernity, and Postmodernism." In *Feminism/Postmodernism*. Ed. Linda Nicholson. New York: Routledge, 1990. 63–82.

Douglas, Mary. *Purity and Danger: An Analysis of the Concepts of Pollution and Taboo*. London: Routledge and Kegan Paul, 1966.

Dyer, Richard. "Male Gay Porn: Coming to Terms." *Jump Cut* no. 30 (1985): 27–29.

———. "White." *Screen* 29. 4 (Autumn 1988): 44–64.

Ebert, Roger. "Why Movie Audiences Aren't Safe Anymore." *American Film* (March 1981): 54–56.

Edelstein, David. "Ward Wields the Cleaver." *Village Voice*. 3 Mar. 1987: 54.

Evans-Pritchard, E.E. *Witchcraft Oracles, and Magic Among the Azande*. London: Oxford UP, 1976.

Foster, Hal. "Postmodernism: A Preface." *The Anti-Aesthetic: Essays on Postmodern Culture*. Ed. Hal Foster. Port Townsend, WA: Bay Press, 1983. ix–xvi.

Fraser, Nancy, and Linda Nicholson. "Social Criticism without Philosophy: An Encounter between Feminism and Postmodernism." In *Feminism/Postmodernism*. Ed. Linda Nicholson. New York: Routledge, 1990. 19–38.

Freud, Sigmund. *Beyond the Pleasure Principle*. [1920] repr. in *The Standard Edition of the Complete Works of Sigmund Freud*. Vol. 18. Trans. James Strachey. London: Hogarth Press, 1961.

———. "Fetishism." [1928] repr. in *The Standard Edition of the Complete Works of Sigmund Freud*. Vol. 21. Trans. James Strachey. London: Hogarth Press, 1961. 152–57.

———. *Introductory Lectures on Psycho-Analysis*. Trans. James Strachey. New York: Norton, 1966.

Friday, Nancy. *My Secret Garden: Women's Sexual Fantasies*. New York: Pocket Books, 1973.

Friedman, Lester. "'Canyons of Nightmare': The Jewish Horror Film." In *Planks of Reason: Essays on the Horror Film*. Ed. Barry Keith Grant. Metuchen, NJ: Scarecrow Press, 1984. 126–52.

Gamman, Lorraine. "Introduction." In *The Female Gaze: Women as Viewers of Popular Culture*. Ed. Lorraine Gamman and Margaret Marshment. Seattle: Real Comet Press. 1–7.

Garfinkel, Harold. *Studies in Ethnomethodology*. Englewood Cliffs, NJ: Prentice Hall, 1967.

Gehr, Richard. "Splatterpunk." *Village Voice*. Feb. 6, 1990: 57–58.

Giles, Dennis. "Conditions of Pleasure in Horror Cinema." In *Planks of Reason: Essays on the Horror Film*. Ed. Barry Keith Grant. Metuchen, NJ: Scarecrow Press, 1984. 38–52.

Gitlin, Todd. "Postmodernism: Roots and Politics." In *Cultural Politics in Contemporary America*. Ed. Ian Angus and Sut Jhally. New York: Routledge, 1989. 347–60.

Grossberg, Lawrence. "Putting the Pop Back into Postmodernism." In *Universal Abandon? The Politics of Post-modernism*. Ed. Andrew Ross. Minneapolis: U of Minnesota P, 1988. 167–90.

Guerrero, Ed. *Framing Blackness: The African American Image in Film*. Philadelphia: Temple UP, 1993.

Halberstam, Judith. *Skin Shows: Gothic Horror and the Technology of Monsters*. Durham, NC: Duke UP, 1995.

Haralovich, Mary Beth. "Sit-coms and Suburbs: Positioning the 1950s Homemaker." In *Private Screenings: Television and the Female Consumer*. Ed. Lynn Spiegel and Denise Mann. Minneapolis: U of Minnesota P, 1992. 110–141.

Hardy, Phil, ed. *The Encyclopedia of Horror Movies*. New York: Harper and Row, 1986.

Hart, Lynda. *Fatal Women: Lesbian Sexuality and the Mark of Aggression*. Princeton: Princeton UP, 1994.

Hinson, Hal. "'Henry': A Killer Cold as Ice." *Washington Post*. 4 May 1990: D7.

Hite, Shere. *The Hite Report*. New York: Macmillan, 1976.

Hutchings, Peter. *Hammer and Beyond: The British Horror Film*. Manchester: Manchester UP, 1993.

Huyssen, Andreas. "Mapping the Postmodern." [1984] repr. in *Feminism/Postmodernism*. Ed. Linda Nicholson. New York: Routledge, 1990. 234–77.

James, Caryn. "'Henry,' the Disturbing, Almost-True Story of a Serial Killer." *New York Times*. 23 Mar. 1990: C12.

Jameson, Fredric. *Postmodernism, or the Cultural Logic of Late Capitalism*. Durham, NC: Duke UP, 1991.

Katz, Jack. *Seductions of Crime: Moral and Sensual Attractions in Doing Evil*. New York: Basic Books, 1988.

King, Stephen. *Danse Macabre*. New York: Berkley Books, 1981.

———. *Pet Sematary*. Garden City, NY: Doubleday, 1983.

Kolodny, Annette. "Dancing Through the Minefield: Some Observations on the Theory, Practice, and Politics of a Feminist Literary Criticism." *Feminist Studies* 6.1 (1980): 1–25.

Kristeva, Julia. *Powers of Horror: An Essay on Abjection*. New York: Columbia UP, 1982.

Lefebvre, Henri. *Everyday Life in the Modern World*. New Brunswick, NJ: Transaction Books, 1984.

Lentz, Kirsten Marthe. "The Popular Pleasures of Female Revenge (or Rage Bursting in a Blaze of Gunfire)." *Cultural Studies* 7 (1993): 374–405.

Levine, Lawrence. *Highbrow/Lowbrow: The Emergence of Cultural Hierarchy in America*. Cambridge: Harvard UP, 1988.

Lucanio, Patrick. *Them or Us: Archetypal Interpretations of Fifties Alien Invasion Films*. Bloomington: Indiana UP, 1987.

Lurie, Susan. "The Construction of the 'Castrated Woman' in Psychoanalysis and Cinema." *Discourse* 4: 52–74.

Lyotard, Jean-François. *The Postmodern Condition: A Report on Knowledge*. Trans. Geoff Bennington and Brian Massumi. Minneapolis: U of Minnesota P, 1984.

Maslin, Janet. "Bloodbaths Debase Movies and Audiences." *New York Times*. 21 Nov. 1982: B1.

McCarty, John. *Splatter Movies: Breaking the Last Taboo of the Screen*. New York: Citadel Press, 1984.

———. *The Modern Horror Film*. New York: Citadel Press, 1990.

McDonough, John. "Director Without a Past." *American Film* (May 1990): 42–45, 49.

Modleski, Tania. "The Terror of Pleasure: The Contemporary Horror Film and Postmodern Theory." *Studies in Entertainment: Critical Approaches to Mass Culture*. Ed. Tania Modleski. Bloomington: Indiana UP, 1986. 155–66.

Movshovitz, Howie. "Henry: Portrait of a Serial Killer." *Denver Post*. 29 June 1990: F6.

Mulvey, Laura. "Visual Pleasure and Narrative Cinema." [1975] repr. in *Movies and Methods, Vol. 2*. Ed. Bill Nichols. Berkeley: U of California P, 1985. 303–15.

———. "Afterthoughts on 'Visual Pleasure and Narrative Cinema' Inspired by *Duel in the Sun* (King Vidor, 1946)." *Framework* no. 15–17 (1981): 12–15.

Neale, Stephen. *Genre*. London: British Film Institute, 1980.

Newman, Kim. *Nightmare Movies: A Critical Guide to Contemporary Horror Films*. New York: Harmony Books, 1988.

———. "Henry: Portrait of a Serial Killer." *Sight and Sound* 1 (July 1991): 43–44.

Owens, Craig. "The Discourse of Others: Feminists and Postmodernism." In *The Anti-Aesthetic: Essays on Postmodern Culture*. Ed. Hal Foster. Port Townsend, WA: Bay Press, 1983. 57–82.

Paul, William. *Laughing Screaming: Modern Hollywood Horror and Comedy*. New York: Columbia UP, 1994.

Pence, Jeffrey. "Terror Incognito: Representation, Repetition, Experience in *Henry: Portrait of a Serial Killer*." *Public Culture* 6 (1994): 525–45.

Pirie, David. *A Heritage of Horror: The English Gothic Cinema 1946–1972*. New York: Equinox Books, 1974.

Pollack, Joe. "Celebration of Murder is Disgusting Exploitation." *St. Louis Post-Dispatch*. 17 Aug. 1990: 3F.

Prince, Stephen. "Dread, Taboo and *The Thing*: Toward a Social Theory of the Horror Film." *Wide Angle* 10.3 (1988): 19–29.

Ringel, Eleanor. "'Henry' Guns for Attention with Serious Murder." *Atlanta Constitution*. 1 June 1990: D1.

Rogin, Michael. "'The Sword Became a Flashing Vision': D. W. Griffith's *The Birth of a Nation*." In *Ronald Reagan, the Movie; And Other Episodes in Political Demonology*. Berkeley: U of California P, 1987. 190–235.

Sanjek, David. "Fans' Notes: The Horror Film Fanzine." *Literature Film Quarterly* 18.3 (1990): 150–59.

Shapiro, Marc. "Wake Up to a New Nightmare." *Fangoria* 137 (Oct. 1994): 40–47.

Sharrett, Christopher. "The Idea of the Apocalypse in *The Texas Chainsaw Massacre*." In *Planks of Reason: Essays on the Horror Film*. Ed. Barry Keith Grant. Metuchen, NJ: Scarecrow Press, 1984. 255–76.

Shelley, Mary. *Frankenstein; or The Modern Prometheus*. [1818] New York: Dell Publishing, 1979.

Sherman, Betsy. "A Killer's Path." *Boston Globe*. 4 Jan. 1990: 7.

Stacey, Jackie. *Star Gazing: Hollywood Cinema and Female Spectatorship*. New York: Routledge, 1994.

Stein, Elliott. "Sexual Adversity in Chicago, *Henry: Portrait of a Serial Killer.*" *Village Voice.* 27 Mar. 1990: 59.

Stern, Michael. "Making Culture into Nature." [1980] repr. in *Alien Zone: Cultural Theory and Contemporary Science Fiction Cinema.* Ed. Annette Kuhn. London: Verso, 1990. 66–72.

Stevenson, Robert Louis. *The Strange Case of Dr. Jekyll and Mr. Hyde.* [1886] Lincoln: U of Nebraska P, 1990.

Stoker, Bram. *Dracula.* [1897] Philadelphia: Running Press, 1995.

Taussig, Michael. *Shamanism, Colonialism and the Wild Man: A Study in Terror and Healing.* Chicago: U of Chicago P, 1987.

———. "Terror as Usual: Walter Benjamin's Theory of History as a State of Siege." *Social Text* 23 (Fall/Winter 1989): 3–20.

Telotte, J.P. "Faith and Idolatry in the Horror Film." *Literature Film Quarterly* 8.3 (1980): 143–55.

———. "The Doubles of Fantasy and the Space of Desire." [1982] repr. in *Alien Zone: Cultural Theory and Contemporary Science Fiction Cinema.* Ed. Annette Kuhn. London: Verso, 1990. 152–59.

Terry, Don. "Chicago Housing Project Basks in a Tense Peace." *New York Times.* 2 Nov. 1992: A10.

Tudor, Andrew. *Monsters and Mad Scientists: A Cultural History of the Horror Movie.* Oxford: Basil Blackwell, 1989.

Twitchell, James. *Dreadful Pleasures: An Anatomy of Modern Horror.* New York: Oxford UP, 1985.

Vale, V., and Andrea Juno, eds. *Incredibly Strange Films* issue of *Re/Search* 10 (1986).

Village Voice. "A Tale from the Crypt." 27 Mar. 1990: 59, 72.

Waller, Gregory. "Introduction." *American Horrors: Essays on the Modern American Horror Film.* Ed. Gregory Waller. Chicago: U of Illinois P, 1987. 1–13.

White, Patricia. "Female Spectator, Lesbian Spector: *The Haunting.*" In *Sexuality and Space.* Ed. Beatriz Colomina. New York: Princeton Architectural Press, 1992. 131–61.

Williams, Linda. "When the Woman Looks." In *Re-Vision: Essays in Feminist Film Criticism*. Ed. Mary Ann Doane, Patricia Mellencamp, and Linda Williams. Frederick, MD: American Film Institute, 1984. 83–99.

———. a *Hard Core: Power, Pleasure and the "Frenzy of the Visible"*. Berkeley: U of California P, 1989.

———. b "Power, Pleasure, and Perversion: Sadomasochistic Film Pornography." *Representations* 27 (Summer, 1989): 37–65.

Williams, Raymond. *The Country and the City*. New York: Oxford UP, 1973.

———. *Marxism and Literature*. New York: Oxford UP, 1977.

Wood, Robin. "Return of the Repressed." *Film Comment* 14.4 (July–Aug. 1978): 25–32.

———. "Cronenberg: A Dissenting View." In *The Shape of Rage: The Films of David Cronenberg*. Ed. Piers Handling. Toronto: General Publishing Co., 1983. 115–35.

———. *Hollywood from Vietnam to Reagan*. New York: Columbia UP, 1986.

FILMS CITED

	Year Released	Director
Abbott and Costello Meet Frankenstein	1948	Charles Barton
Alien	1979	Ridley Scott
Aliens	1986	James Cameron
Alligator	1980	Lewis Teague
Amityville Horror, The	1979	Stuart Rosenberg
Angel Heart	1987	Alan Parker
Anguish	1988	Bigas Luna
Believers, The	1987	John Schlesinger
Birth of a Nation, The	1915	D. W. Griffith
Blackenstein	1973	William Levey
Blacula	1972	William Crain
Blob, The	1958	Irvin Yeaworth
Blood Feast	1963	Herschell Gordon Lewis
Bloodsucking Freaks	1976	Joel Reed
Blue Steel	1990	Kathryn Bigelow
Boyz 'N the Hood	1991	John Singleton
Bride of Frankenstein, The	1935	James Whale
Brood, The	1979	David Cronenberg
Candyman	1992	Bernard Rose
Candyman: Farewell to the Flesh	1995	Bill Condon
Carrie	1976	Brian De Palma
Chopping Mall	1986	Jim Wynorski
Copycat	1995	Jon Amiel
Curse of Frankenstein, The	1957	Terence Fisher

	Year Released	*Director*
Curse of the Werewolf, The	1960	Terence Fisher
Dawn of the Dead	1979	George Romero
Day of the Dead	1985	George Romero
Dead of Night	1945	Alberto Cavalcanti
Demons	1985	Lamberto Bava
Demons 2: The Nightmare Returns	1986	Lamberto Bava
Dr. Black, Mr. Hyde	1976	William Crain
Dr Jekyll and Mr Hyde	1931	Rouben Mamoulian
Dr Jekyll and Sister Hyde	1971	Roy Ward Baker
Dracula	1931	Tod Browning
Dracula	1958	Terence Fisher
Dracula Has Risen From the Grave	1968	Freddie Francis
Dracula's Daughter	1936	Walter Summers
Dressed to Kill	1980	Brian De Palma
Entity, The	1983	Sidney Furie
Evil Dead II: Dead by Dawn	1987	Sam Raimi
Exorcist, The	1973	William Friedkin
Faces of Death	1978	Conan LeCilaire
Fly, The	1958	Kurt Neumann
Fly, The	1986	David Cronenberg
Frankenstein	1931	James Whale
Frankenstein Meets the Wolf Man	1943	Roy William Neill
Freaks	1932	Tod Browning
Friday the 13th	1980	Sean Cunningham
Friday the 13th, Part 2	1981	Steve Miner
Friday the 13th, Part VI: Jason Lives	1986	Tom McLoughlin
Friday the 13th Part 8: Jason Takes Manhattan	1989	Rob Hedden
Ghost of Frankenstein	1942	Erle Kenton
Halloween	1978	John Carpenter
Halloween 2	1981	Rick Rosenthal
Haunting, The	1963	Robert Wise
Headhunter	1989	Francis Schaeffer
Hello Mary Lou: Prom Night II	1987	Bruce Pittman
Henry: Portrait of a Serial Killer (produced in 1986)	1990	John McNaughton

	Year Released	Director
Hills Have Eyes, The	1977	Wes Craven
House of Frankenstein	1944	Erle Kenton
Howling, The	1981	Joe Dante
I Dismember Mama	1974	Paul Leder
I Spit on Your Grave	1977	Mier Zarchi
I Was a Teenage Werewolf	1957	Gene Fowler, Jr.
Invaders from Mars	1953	William Cameron Menzies
Invasion of the Body Snatchers	1956	Don Siegel
King Kong	1933	Merian Cooper and Ernest Schoedsack
Lady in White, The	1988	Frank LaLoggia
Last House on the Left	1972	Wes Craven
March of the Wooden Soldiers	1934	Charles Rogers and Gus Meins
Mark of the Vampire	1935	Tod Browning
Mondo Cane	1963	Gualtiero Jacopetti
Mummy, The	1932	Karl Freund
Mummy's Boys	1936	Fred Guiol
Mummy's Curse, The	1944	Leslie Goodwins
Mummy's Ghost, The	1944	Reginald LeBorg
Mummy's Hand, The	1940	Christy Cabanne
Mummy's Tomb, The	1942	Harold Young
New Nightmare	1994	Wes Craven
Night of the Living Dead	1968	George Romero
Night of the Living Dead	1990	Tom Savini
Nightmare on Elm Street, A	1984	Wes Craven
Nightmare on Elm Street Part 2, A: Freddy's Revenge	1985	Jack Sholder
Nightmare on Elm Street 3, A: Dream Warriors	1987	Chuck Russell
Not of this Earth	1957	Roger Corman
Peeping Tom	1960	Michael Powell
People Under the Stairs, The	1991	Wes Craven
Popcorn	1991	Mark Herrier
Possession of Joel Delaney, The	1972	Waris Hussein
Prophecy	1979	John Frankenheimer
Psycho	1960	Alfred Hitchcock
Q: The Winged Serpent	1982	Larry Cohen

	Year Released	Director
Return of the Vampire	1944	Lew Landers
Rosemary's Baby	1968	Roman Polanski
Scream	1997	Wes Craven
Scream, Blacula, Scream	1973	Bob Kelljan
Serpent and the Rainbow, The	1988	Wes Craven
Silence of the Lambs, The	1991	Jonathan Demme
Sleeping with the Enemy	1991	Joseph Ruben
Slumber Party Massacre, The	1982	Amy Jones
Snuff	1976	Michael and Roberta Findlay
Son of Dracula	1943	Robert Siodmak
Son of Frankenstein	1939	Rowland Lee
Species	1995	Roger Donaldson
Stepfather, The	1987	Joseph Ruben
Stepfather 2: Make Room for Daddy	1989	Jeff Burr
Stepfather 3	1992	Guy Magar
Tales from the Crypt	1972	Freddie Francis
Tales from the Hood	1995	Rusty Cundieff
Targets	1968	Peter Bogdanovich
Terror, The	1963	Roger Corman
Texas Chain Saw Massacre, The	1974	Tobe Hooper
Texas Chain Saw Massacre II, The	1986	Tobe Hooper
Thelma and Louise	1991	Ridley Scott
Them!	1954	Gordon Douglas
They Came from Within	1976	David Cronenberg
Thin Blue Line, The	1988	Errol Morris
Thing, The	1951	Christian Nyby
Thing, The	1982	John Carpenter
Tingler, The	1959	William Castle
Videodrome	1983	David Cronenberg
White Zombie	1932	Victor Halperin
Wizard of Gore, The	1968	Herschell Gordon Lewis
Wolf Man, The	1941	George Waggner
Wolfen	1981	Michael Wadleigh

INDEX